This Book Belongs To:

Thomas Monet Richardson

Tecumseh

AND THE DREAM OF
AN AMERICAN INDIAN NATION

Alvin Josephy's Biography Series of American Indians

Tecumseh

AND THE DREAM OF AN AMERICAN INDIAN NATION

Written by Russell Shorto

INTRODUCTION BY ALVIN M. JOSEPHY, JR.
ILLUSTRATED BY TIM SISCO

Silver Burdett Press

Project editors: Nancy Furstinger (Silver Burdett Press)
Mark Davies & Della Rowland (Kipling Press)
Designed by Mike Hortens

10 9 8 7 6 5 4 3 2 1 (Lib. ed.)
10 9 8 7 6 5 4 3 2 1 (Pbk. ed.)

Library of Congress Cataloging-in-Publication Data

Shorto, Russell.
Tecumseh and the dream of an American Indian nation / by Russell Shorto.
p.   cm. —(Alvin Josephy's biography series of American Indians)
Bibliography: p. 124
1. Tecumseh, Shawnee Chief, 1768–1813—Juvenile literature. 2. Shawnee Indians—
Biography—Juvenile literature. 3. Shawnee Indians—History—Juvenile literature.
4. Indians of North America—Wars—1812–1815—Juvenile literature. 5. Northwest,
Old—History—1776–1865—Juvenile literature. I. Title. II. Series.
E99.S35T34   1989
970.004'97—dc19
[B]   88-32656
CIP
AC
ISBN 0-382-09569-3 (lib. bdg.)
ISBN 0-382-09758-0 (pbk.)

Contents

Introduction *by Alvin M. Josephy, Jr.* vii

Map viii

1. Panther Crouching 1
2. A Shawnee Family 8
3. A Child in Wartime 14
4. Words, Clubs, and Muskets 20
5. The Art of War 29
6. The Lesson of Pontiac 36
7. Fallen Timbers 42
8. A Dying Tradition 49
9. The Rise of the Prophet 57
10. The Warrior Politician 66
11. Distant Thunder 74
12. Prophet Town 79
13. Tecumseh Turns the Tables 85
14. "Sell a Country! Why Not Sell
    the Air?" 90
15. The Battle of Tippecanoe 100
16. War Is Declared 107
17. The Panther's Last Strike 112

Suggested Reading 124

Although this book is based on real events and real people, some dialogue, a few thoughts, and several local descriptions have been reconstructed to make the story more enjoyable. It does not, however, alter the basic truth of the story we are telling.

Unless indicated otherwise, the Indian designs used throughout this book are purely decorative, and do not signify a particular tribe or nation.

Introduction

For 500 years, Christopher Columbus has been hailed as the "discoverer" of America. But Columbus only discovered America for his fellow Europeans, who did not know of its existence. America was really discovered more than 10,000 years before the time of Columbus by people who came across the Bering Strait from Siberia into Alaska. From there they spread south to populate both North and South America. By the time of Columbus, in fact, there were millions of descendants of the true discoverers of America living in all parts of the Western Hemisphere. They inhabited the territory from the northern shores of Alaska and Canada to the southern tip of South America. In what is now the United States, hundreds of tribes, large and small, covered the land from Maine and

Map of
Continental United States
American Indians

MAP BY JIM ROBINSON

Florida to Puget Sound and California. Each tribe had a long and proud history of its own. America was hardly an "unknown world," an "unexplored wilderness"—except to the Europeans who gazed for the first time upon its forests and rivers, its prairies and mountains.

From the very beginning, the newcomers from Europe had many mistaken notions about the people whose ancestors had been living in America for centuries. At first Columbus thought he had reached the East Indies of Asia, and he called the people Indians. The name took hold and remains to this day. But there were more serious misconceptions that had a tragic effect on relations between the Indians and the Europeans. These misconceptions led to one of the greatest holocausts in world history. Indians were robbed of their possessions, their lands, and the lives of countless numbers of their people.

Most Europeans never really understood the thinking, beliefs, values, or religions of the Indians. The Indian way of life was so different from that of the Europeans, who had inherited thousands of years of diverse backgrounds, religions, and ways of thinking and acting. The Europeans looked down on the Indians as strange and different, and therefore inferior. They were ignorant in the way they treated the Indians. To the white people, the Indians were "savages" and "barbarians," who either had to change their ways and become completely like the Europeans or be destroyed.

At the same time, many Europeans came as conquerors. They wanted the Indians' lands and the resources of those lands—resources such as gold, silver, and furs. Their greed, their superior weapons, and their contempt for the Indians' "inferior" ways led to many wars. Of course the Indians fought back to protect the lives of their people, their lands, their religions, their freedoms, their very way of life. But the Europeans—and then their American descendants—assumed that the Indians were all fierce warriors who fought simply because they loved to fight. Only in recent years have we come to see the Indians as they really are—people who would fight when their lives and freedom were at stake. People who were fun-loving children, young lovers, mothers who cried for the safety and health of their families, fathers who did their best to provide food, wise old people who gave advice, religious leaders, philosophers, statesmen, artists, musicians, storytellers, makers of crafts. Yes, and scientists, engineers, and builders of cities as well. The Indian civilizations in Mexico and Peru were among the most advanced the world has ever known.

This book gets beneath the surface of the old, worn-out fables to tell a real story of the Indians—to help us understand how the Indians looked at the world. When we understand this, we can see not only what they did, but why they did it. Everything here is accurate history, and it is an exciting story. And it is told in such a way that we, the readers, can imagine ourselves back among the Indians of the past, identifying ourselves with their ways of life, beliefs, and destinies. Perhaps in the end we will be able to ask: What choices would we have had? How would we ourselves have responded and behaved?

The story of the great Shawnee Indian chief Tecumseh has fascinated Americans for generations. Tecumseh was a bold and talented warrior. But he was also a respected statesman, a powerful and persuasive speaker, and a man who cared about other human beings. This was true at a time when the relations between Indians and whites on the western border of the young United States were very strained.

Tecumseh dreamed of a united Indian nation that would flourish in our present-day Midwest. In many ways he worked very hard to bring it about. In doing so, he had a shrewd understanding of the white people's politics. He knew how to use the Europeans' ways to his advantage. If he had not been killed fighting for the British in the War of 1812, there is no telling what he might have accomplished. Certainly, the United States never again met an Indian foe with the grand sweep of his vision. If he had lived, there is every reason to believe that he would have been the one Indian leader who could have created an Indian State.

—Alvin M. Josephy, Jr.

1

Panther Crouching

A swarthy, grim-faced Indian stood on the bank of the Detroit River gazing across the water at a sturdy and heavily stockaded wooden fort. The Indian wore deerskin leggings and moccasins. His bare chest and shoulders rippled with muscles as his hands clenched the barrel of a musket. Two feathers stuck out from the top of his head.

He was Pontiac, chief of the Ottawa Indians, the proudest and most independent chief of his day, and the most skillful warrior. His impending mission seemed impossible, even for him: to attack the solid and well-manned Fort Detroit and take it from the British.

The year was 1763 and the French and Indian War—the great war between England and France for control of North America—was over, but the fighting was not. The English had defeated the French and their Indian allies and now claimed not only the East Coast with its bustling cities and towns, but the wide, rich lands westward as well. The British moved in and took over the old French trade routes. From now on the Indians had to trade their furs with the English.

The British did not treat the Indians as well as the French had, however. They cheated the Indians in their business deals and established forts and towns on land that belonged to the Indians. The haughty British believed that the Indians were too divided and weak to oppose them.

But they did not know about Pontiac. This great, fearless chief was also a skillful organizer. He had gathered together the chiefs of eighteen tribes. His plan was to convince them that by uniting and fighting under his leadership they could defeat the British invaders. Dozens of chiefs and warriors from the Hurons, Ottawas, Shawnee, and many other tribes sat in a huge circle around a brightly leaping campfire. Standing before them, his eyes burning as hot as the fire, Pontiac spoke in a voice that rang through the forest:

"My brothers, we must exterminate from our land this nation which seeks to kill us! We can no longer get supplies from the French; and the Englishmen sell merchandise at twice the cost and their goods are worth nothing. When I tell the English chief that some of our warriors are dead, he does not weep for the dead as the French used to do, but makes fun of me! When I ask him for something for our sick, he refuses and tells me that he has no need of us. You can well see that he seeks our ruin. Well, my brothers, we must all swear to ruin them!"

Pontiac's words convinced the chiefs to join him in attacking the British. Under his guidance, thousands of determined braves ravaged forts and settlements throughout the Old Northwest—the lands of present-day Michigan, Wisconsin, Indiana, Ohio, and western Pennsylvania. They took scalps and left a trail of corpses and charred buildings.

The Indians fought ferociously because, as Pontiac had helped them to recognize, the British troops and English-speaking settlers moving inland were causing terrible destruction. In many parts of the country, they were driving Indians from their villages, seizing their gardens and hunting grounds, killing their women, children, and old people, and desecrating the Indian burial places. The white men were a threat to the Indians' way of life. They had to be stopped. So Pontiac's alliance attacked forts throughout the Old Northwest, and the British troops fled in terror.

But Pontiac's attack on Fort Detroit, the strongest British fort, failed. Pontiac was forced to order his braves to retreat into the forest, where they could rest and nurse their wounds. Afterward, he met with the British commander and informed him that the siege was over. "All my braves have buried their hatchets," he said.

Even so, the Indians remained strong in the western lands. The attacks were less frequent, but they continued. At last, King George made a deal that was meant to settle the conflict. The British proclaimed a boundary along the Appalachian Mountains, running from western Pennsylvania south through lands now called West Virginia, Kentucky, and Tennessee. No white settlers would be allowed to cross it. This would keep the whites in the east and would set aside the western lands as a permanent Indian territory.

Pontiac accepted these terms. The chiefs of the other tribes joyously agreed that this was the best resolution they could have hoped for. Fighting ceased. The warriors returned to their wigwams with the good news that their troubles were over.

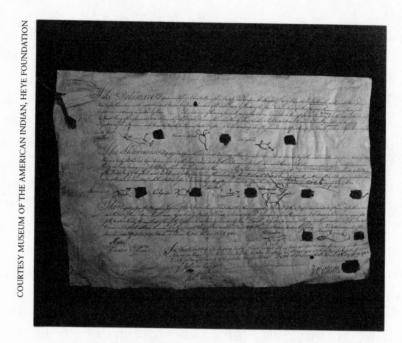

1765 Treaty between the British and the Indians

The alliance of Indian tribes against the white man had been successful. Peace was here to stay.

But King George was a long distance away in England. To his dismay, he found that he didn't have much influence over the American colonists. The lush, fertile lands west of the mountains were too tempting for them to ignore. They kept crossing into these lands, despite the proclamation; and they hacked hundreds of acres of trees to clear fields for their farms.

Wealthy landowners claimed whole forests for their plantations. One of these men, George Washington, who would one day be the first president of a new nation, wrote: "I can never look upon that proclamation in any other light than as a temporary expedient to quiet the minds of the Indians, which must fall, of course, in a few years." So the settlers were not doing as the British government had ordered. It seemed to many that some day these upstart American colonists would clash with their English rulers.

The settlers continued to spread deeper into the forbidden lands of Ohio, Kentucky, and Tennessee. The forests rang with their musket shots as they slaughtered deer, bear, pheasants, and turkeys—not just for food, but often simply for sport.

The Indians, who had believed the British when they told them no whites would cross the mountains into their lands, gazed with anger and frustration upon the ruined forests and butchered animals. These forests were their homes. They had always used them wisely and hunted only those animals they needed. They could not comprehend why these newcomers, whom the Indians called Long Knives because of the big hunting knives they carried, seemed to love destroying nature.

The great Pontiac had failed after all in his attempt to unite the tribes and hold the white men back. The Indians wondered what they could do. Would a new leader emerge? Who would he be? Where would he come from?

* * *

The year was 1768. It was a deliciously crisp and silent night in the Ohio region. The March sky was thick with stars. The forest surrounding the Shawnee village of Old Piqua mirrored the peaceful atmosphere.

The only sound came from a small, dome-shaped wigwam covered with elm bark. It was a tiny place, just big enough to hold three adults. This was the birth house, specially built for Shawnee women who were about to give birth. As Pontiac, away to the north, was realizing that his great war had not stopped the white man, here in the forests of Ohio a baby was being born.

Inside the birth house, lying on a big, furry bearskin, a small woman sweated and strained. With her were the village

Tecumseh's namesake - Panther Crouching

medicine man and a midwife. Outside, the woman's husband, Puckeshinwa, chief of the village, waited nervously. The medicine man's hand was on the woman's swollen belly, his head cocked intently.

Suddenly, he nodded and, in one movement, he and the midwife lifted the pregnant woman to her feet and helped her into a squatting position. In the next instant the woman let out a scream and her child, a boy, was delivered right into her waiting hands. This was the Shawnee way of giving birth.

At the same moment the midwife, looking through the doorway, cried out and pointed to the sky directly overhead. A bright star shot across the heavens and vanished. Puckeshinwa, the new father, gazed at the wondrous sight. Then he stuck his head inside the birth house. He and his wife, Methoataske, smiled at one another. Immediately after a child's birth, the Shawnee always looked to nature for a sign by which to name the new infant. Here was a very good one indeed. In Shawnee religion, a shooting star represented a panther. The woman immediately chose her son's name: Tecumtha, which meant "Panther Crouching." Chief Puckeshinwa nodded. It was a good name.

For the time being, "crouching" was a good term for the infant boy. But in years to come this panther—this Tecumtha, whom the white men would come to know as Tecumseh— would do more than crouch. One day, when he had developed into an awesome leader, he would pounce on the white invaders, and they would learn to fear his terrible claws.

꒒꒒꒒꒒꒒ **2** ꒒꒒꒒꒒꒒

A Shawnee Family

Tecumseh grew rapidly. As a boy he was sleek and wiry in build. His deep brown eyes took in all that happened and sparkled with sharp intelligence. At a very early age he began to show the promise of a great warrior. At five he killed his first rabbit and solemnly handed it to his mother to add to the family's cooking pot. At six he had fashioned his own hunting club from a stout hickory branch, a rock twice as big as his fist, and a deerskin sack.

He made his club in the Shawnee way. He wet the deerskin sack and then wrapped it around the stone and tied it with a tough leather tong through a hole in the bottom of the stick. Then he heated the deerskin over the fire. As it dried, the skin tightened around the stone. When the club was finished, he decorated it with feathers.

With this club, Tecumseh amazed the whole village by felling his first deer at the age of seven. Spotting his prey, the young hunter posed his body as skillfully as an adult, bent his arm, and sent the club flying with one swift movement. It flew true, and struck the young deer in the head. Tecumseh returned to the village triumphant.

Shawnee maple war club

None of the Shawnee had ever heard of a boy so young with the stealth, accuracy, and strength necessary to kill a deer. The only one who wasn't surprised was his older brother, Chiksika. He had trained Tecumseh daily and knew of the boy's quick mind and agile young body.

The wigwam of Puckeshinwa and Methoataske was large and bustling. By now seven-year-old Tecumseh had several brothers and sisters. One of his older sisters, Tecumpease, was a loving, bright-eyed young woman who cared for and watched over the other children, while Chiksika, Tecumseh's older brother, was fourteen and already a brave warrior. Most of the noise these days was caused by the triplets that Methoataske had recently given birth to.

News of this event reached beyond Old Piqua to every Shawnee village in Ohio, for twins were very rare and not even the oldest Shawnees could recall a birth of triplets. Not long after their birth, one of the three boys died, leaving the other two who were named Kumskaukau and Lalawethika.

Tecumseh's family was a close and happy one. Methoataske and her daughters worked in the village's vegetable fields, tending the pumpkins, squash, beans, and corn. They also sewed clothing for everyone in the family. Puckeshinwa and Chiksika rode with the other men of the village to the tribal hunting grounds. After many days they would return with their horses straining under the weight of their dressed elk and deer.

In the warm months the family lived in a large, comfortable wigwam. It covered twenty square feet and was made of strips of bark stretched over supporting poles. The roof had two slanting sides that peaked in the center, as in the houses of the white settlers. The inside was one large room where the family ate and slept, and where Tecumseh and his little brothers played on rainy days. Just in front of the wigwam there was a group of log seats where Puckeshinwa would sit on hot summer evenings notching his arrowheads while Methoataske sewed buckskin into clothing.

In the winter, the family moved to a smaller, dome-shaped wigwam. The hearth was in the center of the one small room, and there was a hole in the ceiling for letting the smoke out. All the family would cluster around the fire in the evenings, sitting on bearskins and listening to the winter wind howl outside. In the morning, Tecumseh would wake up and lift the thick hide that served as the door. Outside snow would be drifting high around the bases of the trees. Tecumseh loved the winter for its magical white snowfalls that hushed the forest, just as he loved the summer for its sultry warmth, the spring for its crackling newness and life, and the fall for its rich colors and swollen harvest of crops.

For the boy Tecumseh, each season brought new adventures. He and his family worked, played, and grew together. For a time after the birth of the triplets, life was perfect for the family of Puckeshinwa and Methoataske.

But in their cities of the east, the white settlers of America had grown tired of British rule and were more anxious than before to strike into the rich, forbidden lands of the west. Life was about to change for the happy family.

* * *

Puckeshinwa was a member of the Kispokotha, the division of the Shawnee most noted for their skills in war. As war chief, he had aided Pontiac by leading the Shawnee of the Ohio Valley southward into the forests of Virginia to battle the settlers there. Unlike many Indians, though, Puckeshinwa was not hopeful that the British proclamation would bring peace for the tribes. In his lifetime he had ranged far along the borders of the territories of the Long Knives, and he had seen evidence of their ravenous hunger for land. He could not believe that these men would submit to being bound by a piece of paper signed by a king thousands of miles across the water.

As it turned out, Puckeshinwa was right. One spring day in 1774, he and some other Shawnee warriors crouched amid the new growth in their old hunting forests in Kentucky and watched as a stream of wagons rolled in, carrying Virginia colonists eager to expand their farms.

The leader of this party was a man named John Floyd. His mission was to bring the party to the Ohio River, where the men, most of whom were land surveyors, were to mark out boundaries for themselves or for wealthy patrons who had commissioned them to do so. One of the surveyors had been commissioned by George Washington to mark off the choicest land. Another was employed by Patrick Henry, the Virginia patriot who for several years had been urging his fellow colonists to revolt against British rule.

The colonists were not deterred

Puckeshinwa's warriors decided to teach these men that they would be wise to follow the rules of their king. Sweeping down on them with piercing war cries, they swiftly surrounded the wagons. Before the white men knew what was happening, their wagons, containing all their valuable surveying equipment, were in flames and they were prisoners. After a short time the Indians released their captives and allowed them to return to their people to spread the word of what awaited any who ventured into the hunting grounds of the Shawnee.

But the colonists were not deterred. They began to move into the westward lands in larger groups and armed for war. By October a unit of 1,000 militiamen had gathered on the banks of the Ohio River. There they awaited the arrival of two other units. Then they would all march on the Shawnee.

The war chief of all the Shawnee, Cornstalk, was too wise to allow this to happen. He rapidly gathered several hundred

Shawnee braves to battle the colonists' army before it grew stronger. In the Shawnee war party were Puckeshinwa and his eldest son, fourteen-year-old Chiksika. Cornstalk planned to surprise the enemy while it was camped across the river. He marched his men several miles upstream from the enemy camp and there they silently crossed the river. Once across, they were to slip into the camp and attack while the white men slept.

But two lookouts spotted the approaching Indians and sounded the alarm. The pre-dawn forest became alive with the crack of musket fire and cries of agony. Puckeshinwa and Chiksika, fighting side by side, advanced steadily through the fire until Puckeshinwa suddenly clutched his side and dropped to the earth. In terror, the young Chiksika fell beside his father and tried to examine the wound. But the aging war chief pushed his hand aside.

"It is a bad wound," Puckeshinwa whispered. Then he looked sternly into the frightened eyes of his young son. Suddenly, the boy knew his father was about to die. Quickly, Puckeshinwa made Chiksika understand that he was now the man of his family. He, Chiksika, would have to care for his mother, his older sisters, and his younger brothers. Chiksika nodded.

Puckeshinwa had his son promise that he would never sign a treaty with the white man and that he would fight the Long Knives with his last ounce of strength. Chiksika also promised to train Tecumseh to follow the same path. With that, Puckeshinwa's eyes closed. A gurgling gasp of air left his throat, and he was dead.

3
A Child in Wartime

So Chiksika took over Tecumseh's training. As the child grew, both his brother, Chiksika, and their mother, Methoataske, kept the image of his father, and especially of his death at the hands of the white men, alive in his young mind.

Tecumseh idolized his older brother, and he in turn was Chiksika's favorite. They became inseparable, doing everything together. Chiksika was the most dashing and daring of the young Shawnee warriors. He was short, but built solidly, with legs that powerfully gripped his horse's sides when he led an attack, and arms that could swing a war club with terrifying force. He was also a good-natured young man and devoted to his family and tribe. He was the perfect teacher, and young Tecumseh hung on his every word.

Chiksika taught Tecumseh not only hunting, but the ways of war. The image of the death of Puckeshinwa was never absent from Tecumseh's mind. At night he vowed to the Great Spirit, the protector of the Shawnee in the spirit world, that he would train himself to become a great warrior. He would avenge the death of his father and of the thousands of Indians who had fallen at the hands of the white invaders.

In time, Tecumseh became the leader of the other children in the village. The adults smiled at his youthful zest. Using the knowledge of warfare that Chiksika had taught him, Tecumseh began staging elaborate battles among the children. Chiksika had told his brother all the details of the Battle of Point Pleasant, at which their father had died. Now, standing in the village with some friends, Chiksika was amazed to see the boys and girls acting out the battle down to the smallest detail, while young Tecumseh directed—playing the part not of his father but of Cornstalk.

Even Chiksika, who knew his brother better than anyone, was amazed at how carefully Tecumseh had listened to the details of the battle, and at how devotedly the Shawnee children followed Tecumseh's orders. Chiksika realized that his young brother had the makings not only of a great warrior, but of a chief among chiefs.

* * *

When Tecumseh was eight years old and leading parties of pretend Shawnee warriors against parties of pretend white soldiers, an event occurred 300 miles to the east that was to change the future of the Shawnee and of the whole North American continent. In that year, 1776, in the city of Philadelphia a gathering of American colonists—most of them wealthy, middle-aged landowners—signed a piece of paper that they called the Declaration of Independence.

The Shawnee could no longer think of all white men as the same. Those whose homes were in America and who were now calling themselves Americans had split off from the mother country, England. With the signing of the Declaration of Independence, war officially broke out between these two groups of white men. The Shawnee and the other Indian tribes realized that they had to take a stand on the Revolutionary War. Would they fight with one side against the other, or would they remain neutral and let the whites fight it out among themselves?

It didn't take the Shawnee long to reach a decision. In the French and Indian War, they had fought against the British. The French who were in North America were mostly traders who lived as the Indians did. The Shawnee understood them and their ways. But the British were red-coated foreigners who marched haughtily through the forests as if they owned them. Now most Shawnee chose to side with the British, not because they had any love for them, but because they sensed that if the Americans won their independence, their first move would be to expand into the western lands. The loss of Indian land had

Shawnee drum

to be prevented at all costs. Soon Shawnee war parties were teaming up with units of British soldiers.

For a time, the fighting was carried out in the east, far from Shawnee lands. But in 1779, things changed. One morning, a scout on horseback galloped into Tecumseh's sleepy village with the news that hundreds of white soldiers were headed toward them, shooting and killing Indians as they went. The villagers flew to action. The women packed supplies, and the men rushed for their arms. They barely had time to react, though, before the first of the mounted American soldiers, dressed in the leather jerkins of mountain men, burst through the trees with their muskets blazing.

Methoataske huddled in the family wigwam with her daughters and the young boys. Chiksika grabbed his musket and ordered Tecumseh to stay with the family. He started to run off, but spun around when he saw his brother following him.

"No!" he cried, and in his voice was a steely tone that Tecumseh had never heard him use before. It was the tone of battle, a tone that was to be obeyed. Chiksika pointed to the wigwam. "Protect!" he cried, then ran off to help the other warriors.

For a moment Tecumseh wavered, then he turned and went into the wigwam. In battle, he knew, a warrior must follow orders. Picking up the musket Chiksika had recently given to him, he crouched at the wigwam door and kept guard over his family.

The Shawnee defeated the soldiers and sent them running, but many in the village were frightened at how close the white men's war had suddenly come. After much debate, nearly 1,000 Shawnee decided to move farther west to the land of Missouri to escape the warfare.

Chiksika argued vehemently that the Shawnee should not run from their lands but should stay and protect them. Therefore, he, his brothers, and his sister Tecumpease stayed behind. Their mother, Methoataske, and one sister went west. The family hoped that the war would end soon and they would be reunited shortly. Tecumseh hugged his mother and watched her depart. He had no idea that he would never see her again. The war would last several more years, and by the time it was over she would be dead.

Tecumpease—now a lovely, gentle-voiced young woman of nineteen took over the care of the family. She and Chiksika were like mother and father to their younger brothers. She loved and cared for them all, but she was especially fond of Tecumseh, who hunted as skillfully as a man and whose hearty laughter rang through the village and cheered her on rainy days. She took special care mending his moccasins and caring for the scrapes and bruises he always seemed to have when he returned from a hunting trip with his friends. She saw that he quickly learned the beliefs and traditions of the Shawnee, especially the strict Shawnee code of honesty.

The white man's war had split the Shawnee and now they were widely scattered. Though some of the young warriors like Chiksika would have liked to break all ties with the whites, this was impossible. Over the years the Shawnee had become dependent on the goods sold by French and British traders. Such items as metal pots, knives, and guns and bullets had become vital to the Shawnee. They couldn't imagine how they could live without them. Thus, while the whites were their bitterest enemies, they were also the suppliers of things the Indians needed.

At night Chiksika would sit with his brothers and sister around the family fire and tell them how he believed it was necessary for the Indians to break with the whites no matter how difficult it was. Young Tecumseh's heart was already that of a warrior, and he renewed his pledge to fight to avenge Shawnee deaths. He now added a pledge to fight for a return to the Shawnee traditions. Chiksika stared at his brother's determined face and smiled, wondering what part his brother would play in securing the future of his people.

Chiksika then stared at his youngest brothers, now five years old. Kumskaukau was an average little boy. No doubt he would grow into an average warrior who would follow orders and fight as diligently as he could. But the other boy, Lalawethika, was difficult to figure out. He was always getting into trouble—tripping, knocking things over, crying, kicking, and scattering the embers of the fire. Even his name meant Noise Maker. What kind of adult would this rambunctious little one grow into?

4

Words, Clubs, and Muskets

Shouted orders and cries of pain filled the air. Bullets sputtered in the dirt and cracked through the low-hanging branches, sending showers of twigs down on the line of Shawnee warriors. Ahead, through the bitter-tasting smoke of gunpowder blasts, fourteen-year-old Tecumseh could see the enemy. There seemed to be hundreds of white men in buckskin jackets and raccoon caps, each with one eye squinting along the barrel of a musket that was aimed right at him.

Suddenly, the boy heard a cry and saw to his horror the two rows of soldiers jump to their feet and dash through the thicket toward the Indians. Chiksika, who was leading the Shawnee against the invading Kentucky militiamen, cried for his men to hold their positions. The Indians lay flat against the ground and fired through the smoke at the rushing enemy. They knew the militiamen had to be nearly upon them, but they couldn't see a thing.

All at once a great grizzled white face, covered with hair like the face of an animal, appeared before Tecumseh. The man had apparently run out of ammunition and so was swinging his rifle like a club. His eyes bulged with fury and his deep voice was bellowing like a bear's. He caught sight of Tecumseh and made straight for him.

Tecumseh runs from battle

Without realizing what he was doing, Tecumseh leaped to his feet, threw his musket at the massive form, and fled back into the woods. Bullets skipped around him but he ran on. He came to the Mad River, which the Shawnee were trying to prevent the soldiers from crossing, and ran along the bank. He ran for miles, until he dropped to the ground from exhaustion.

A short while later he opened his eyes. At once his whole being was filled with self-hatred. He knew what he was: a deserter. His brother had granted him permission to join the warriors in his first battle, and he had deserted. Not only that, but he had deserted the very line his brother was commanding, his brother whom he admired more than anyone. There was nothing left for him to do but continue running, north or south or west, it didn't matter. But never again could he face Chiksika.

A few hours later, however, Tecumseh had found his way back to his brother's company of warriors. He had just made the hardest decision in his young life: to return and face punishment. He had had a long argument with himself and at the end of it he was left with one realization. As a Shawnee and his father's son, there was no place on Earth for him but alongside Shawnee warriors fighting for their land and customs. If he couldn't do that, he would face punishment as a Shawnee.

Chiksika had been wounded in the battle. When Tecumseh saw the blood-soaked binding around his brother's arm, his face burned with shame. Why hadn't he stayed and helped his brother? Solemnly, Tecumseh presented himself to Chiksika and in stern, powerful words told of his desertion. He did not try to make excuses. In fact, he claimed that the reason he had fled was pure cowardice.

"I do not deserve to be a warrior among the Shawnee," he said. The voice was not that of a boy. His words were sharp and sure. Bowing his head, he finished by saying he would accept whatever punishment his leader named.

Chiksika and the other warriors listened to the firm, serious voice of this youth. Every one of them felt how deeply ashamed the boy was. Chiksika bade the boy look him in the eyes. Then, speaking as formally and solemnly as had his young brother, he pronounced his punishment: The warrior Tecumseh was to be banished forever from the Shawnee tribes . . . if he ever again deserted in battle. In one's first battle such panic was understandable, and it would be forgiven, but never again.

Tecumseh started to protest, claiming that he didn't deserve a second chance. But Chiksika silenced him with a cold glance. He, the chief and leader of the war party, had spoken. It was the warrior's place to obey. Then Chiksika's creased mouth softened into a smile.

"The next time, my brother, you will do well," he assured him.

"I will," Tecumseh promised, "or I will die trying."

* * *

Tecumseh's next chance came soon. The Shawnee's main activity during the Revolutionary War was harassing the American flatboats that punted up and down the Ohio River. The flatboats were like enormous covered rafts that the patriot troops used to transport kegs of gunpowder, muskets, food, and men.

One day not long after Tecumseh's first battle, scouts slipped into the village to report sighting half a dozen flatboats on the Ohio River, heading south into Kentucky. According to the old British proclamation and to the Shawnee, this was Indian land.

Immediately, Chiksika assembled a small party of warriors to ambush the boats. One of the first he turned to was Tecumseh. Tecumseh's heart burned with gratitude toward his brother for selecting him. This time, he told himself, he would not disappoint Chiksika.

The Indians reached the bank just in time to see the boats float into view around a bend. Tecumseh, the sleek young panther, crouched in the brush alongside the bank and gazed on the enemy. He had already forgotten the past, and was busy calculating the strength of the enemy and how the attack might best be executed. Although Chiksika had taught him much of warfare, already the boy's tactical instincts were beyond those of his experienced brother.

Chiksika whispered in consultation with the older warriors. They suggested that several of the Indians float out into the middle of the river concealed behind driftwood while the others began the attack from the shore.

"No!"

The warriors looked around and there sat Tecumseh. He simply couldn't hold himself back. Didn't they see how foolhardy it would be to leave men nearly helpless in the water? What if they were discovered? Before Chiksika could quiet him, he blurted out his own plan. A half mile downstream the river narrowed and the far bank became dangerously shallow. There, the boats would be forced to move closer to the Indians' side. That would be the best place to attack, and it wouldn't require sending men out into the water.

Chiksika looked at his brother and smiled. "It is a better plan," he told the others, and they nodded and looked at the boy.

The warriors managed to get downstream to where the river narrowed just as the flatboats did. At once Chiksika motioned for attack, and the muskets opened fire on the soldiers while flaming arrows whizzed through the air and struck the cargo. The air around Tecumseh filled with acrid smoke and the shouts of battle. This time, though, there was no fear in him. It was as though the first battle had burned all confusion from his system. Now everything seemed clear. The taste of the smoke was not strange and fearful, but sharp and clean. It was the taste of glory.

The boats fell into disorder, some punting faster to try to escape the rain of bullets and arrows while others maneuvered for fighting space. Two were burning out of control. A man on the first boat, obviously the leader of the party, barked a series of orders. The boats ponderously worked into a battle line and the soldiers, taking cover behind boxes, began returning the Indians' fire. Now it was a standoff between the two sides.

Chiksika sent Tecumseh and two other warriors upriver to the last boat to attack it more directly. One of the warriors lit an arrow, but Tecumseh stopped him. He wanted to try to take this boat. Upon Tecumseh's instructions, his companions opened fire with their muskets and peppered the boat with bullets. Tecumseh, meanwhile, crept down to the water and slipped silently beneath the surface.

He swam underwater the ten yards to the boat, then ducked underneath it and came up on the other side, behind the soldiers, who were facing their enemy on the riverbank. Catlike, Tecumseh slithered onto the boat. His buckskin leggings were dripping and his muscular chest glistened with water. He silently slid up behind the nearest soldier and buried his tomahawk in the man's skull. Another soldier heard the sick thud and spun around aiming his gun. Tecumseh had no musket. He pushed a crate at the man. It knocked him off balance, and Tecumseh leapt over the crates stacked between them and hacked the man's head nearly off.

Looking around quickly, Tecumseh saw that there was only one more soldier alive on the boat, and he was in the ridiculous position of being out of ammunition while using a crate of bullets for protection. For a moment the man thought of pulling out his knife and going hand to hand with this Indian who looked so young that he couldn't be very experienced. But a glance at his companions, lying in pools of their own blood, made him think better of it. Carefully, the man pulled out his knife and dropped it to the ground. Tecumseh nodded and pointed toward shore.

A few minutes later, the boat ground ashore just ahead of the Indians' position. The other flatboats had burned on the water or escaped. When Tecumseh stepped off with his prisoner, he was mobbed by his fellow warriors offering congratulations. Chiksika's eyes were brighter than Tecumseh had ever seen them, bright with pride. Tecumseh bent his head to show humility before the chief.

"We have a boat!" a warrior cried.

"And a prisoner!" another shouted, and they all cheered, seeming especially happy over this. Tecumseh wondered why having a prisoner was such a great thing, unless it was to get information out of him. A short while later, when the warriors had marched to a stream and made camp, he found out.

They stacked wood for a huge fire, and in the center they posted a large log upright. The prisoner was tied to the log, and then the fire was lit. Terror flashed into the man's eyes, and his cries of agony rose with the licking flames. The Indians laughed at the sight and pointed out to each other how undignified the white man was in the face of pain. An Indian would never cry out so.

Tecumseh watched in horror. At fifteen, he was the youngest present and had no right to question his elders. But he had been taught by his mother and his sister Tecumpease the right and wrong of things. Even in warfare, he knew, there were things that were wrong. And this was surely one of them. Tecumseh did not know that while the Shawnee practiced a strict code of morals, in warfare their traditions were of the utmost cruelty. Burning prisoners alive just to see them die was accepted as a form of entertainment following a successful battle.

The flames leapt higher and the man's screams had now become inhuman, like a voice from the spirit world. If it was from the spirit world, Tecumseh thought, it was crying to the Shawnee for decency. With a shudder, Tecumseh thought that it might be the voice of the Great Spirit himself. Yes, that was it! This was the Great Spirit crying out to them in pain. By viciously murdering a helpless prisoner they were making fun of life. They were showing the Great Spirit that the Shawnee had no respect for life.

If this was an example of how the Shawnee treated living beings, was it any wonder that the Great Spirit was allowing the whites to take their lands, kill their animals, and destroy their traditions? Surely, the Great Spirit would only help and protect them if they helped and protected those who were defenseless.

Without another thought, Tecumseh jumped into the center of the flames and hacked the tough cords that bound the prisoner to the log. His companions jumped to their feet in alarm. Tecumseh pulled the blackened form from the fire, but he could see he was too late. The man had stopped crying out a moment before, and now he was dead.

"Tecumseh, what is the meaning of this?" It was Chiksika, standing before him.

Tecumseh gently laid the prisoner's body on the ground and stood up. His own arms were burned from holding the corpse.

"Are we any better than the white men?" he cried to his brother and the others. Chiksika stared at him. He had never heard such a tone in his younger brother. It was a voice that boomed through the dark forest and echoed in the walls of one's mind. It was not the voice of an Indian boy who respected his elders, but of an Indian chief or priest who was ashamed of his followers.

"Do we fight to save our lands," Tecumseh went on, "or for the love of murder? The Great Spirit gave this land to his red children. Now the white men are driving us from it. They do not believe in the Great Spirit. But do we Shawnee respect the Great Spirit? Do we respect life? Do we have hearts and minds or are we lower than animals?"

Tecumseh raged, his voice growing deeper and more passionate as he talked. The warriors stared and listened as if it were the voice of their ancestors talking to them with the wisdom of the ages. When Tecumseh was finished, the warriors hung their heads. Chiksika, too, felt shame burn his insides.

Now silent, Tecumseh seemed to come back to himself, just as he had returned to himself following his flight from his first battle. Only now, instead of stewing in shame, he thought about the words that had come from his mouth. He knew them to be true.

He had just discovered a powerful truth that he would never forget: Words could have as much power as clubs or muskets.

5
The Art of War

The year was 1787 and in the East the Revolutionary War was over. The American colonists had at last overthrown the British rule. Representatives of the thirteen colonies, now called states, were meeting in Philadelphia to draw up a constitution that would contain the basic laws of their new nation. As colonists, they had been upset by unjust treatment from the British. Now they were determined to set up laws that would ensure liberty and justice for all people.

But once again the native Americans were to be left out. The new government wanted the rich western lands from the moment it assumed power. In fact, many of the new leaders were the same landowners who had claimed vast tracts of Indian land for themselves.

After the war, the new government claimed the western lands, naming the region the Northwest Territory. It included the future states of Ohio, Indiana, Illinois, Michigan and Wisconsin, and part of Minnesota. Government land managers also divided up the territories of Kentucky and Tennessee. The government then began forcing many of the Indian tribes in these areas to sign "land cession" treaties in which the Indians promised to give up large sections of their land in exchange for supplies. Much of the land in Ohio surrounding Tecumseh's homelands was given by the government to its war veterans as payment for their military service.

The British, meanwhile, had been forced out of the new country, but not off the continent. Canada was still loyal to England, so many British troops and traders moved northward. From there, British traders would range south to sell their wares to the Indians in exchange for furs. At each village they visited, the traders told the Indians how land-hungry the new American government was and how President George Washington would not be content until the whole continent belonged to the United States and all the Indian tribes had been wiped out.

These traders may have exaggerated their tales, but for the most part they told the truth and the Indians knew it. The Indians who had signed treaties were not important chiefs, but small ones who had no right to speak for their tribes. Although many important Shawnee chiefs, such as the aging Black Hoof, were not pleased by the signing of the treaties, they wanted very much to have peace with the strong new country. They counseled their warriors to accept what had been done.

But Chiksika and Tecumseh were infuriated when they learned of the signing of these treaties. Swiftly gathering those braves who were prepared to die to save Indian lands, the two brothers sped southward to battle the troops that were moving into the old hunting grounds. In Tennessee the Shawnee met

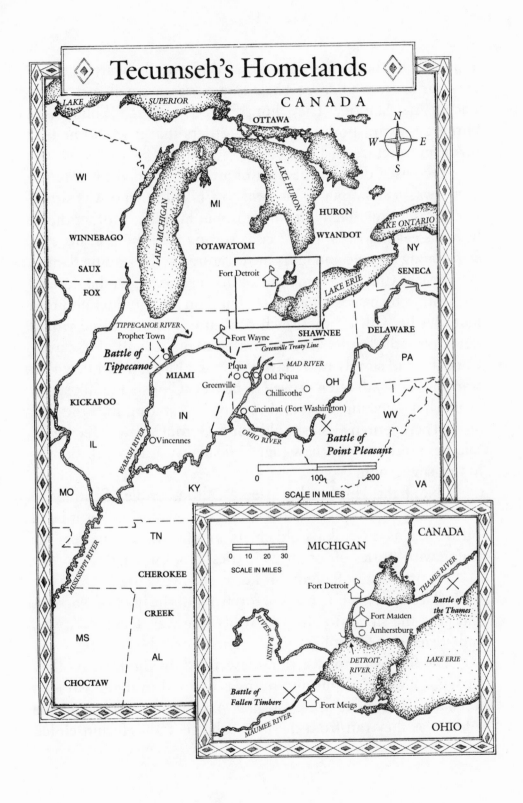

Tecumseh's Homelands

a party of Cherokee, who were also on the warpath, and they formed an alliance. Their target was a small fort called Buchanan's Station. They hoped to do enough killing and burning to warn both troops and settlers that it would be best for them to return east.

Tecumseh devised the plan of attack. The night before the battle was to take place, he went to Chiksika, who was sitting by the campfire, to tell him about it. But his older brother didn't hear his eager words. He just sat staring into the fire, his eyes envisioning strange and fantastic creatures in the leaping flames.

At last Chiksika came out of his reverie. When he noticed his brother by his side, he put his hand on his shoulder and told him that he had felt the touch of death. Tomorrow, he would not survive the battle. Tecumseh tried to make light of it, saying Chiksika had simply been daydreaming, although he knew that warnings of death often proved to be true. Chiksika didn't speak again, but only shrugged and returned to staring into the fire.

"Then perhaps you should not fight tomorrow," Tecumseh said hesitantly, for he knew that Chiksika would not take kindly to this suggestion.

"Not fight!" his brother cried. "Our father died fighting the whites. It is a glorious end. If I am to die, I would rather it be in battle than as a wrinkled old chieftain who sits and pesters the young with stories of forgotten battles. No, I will fight."

As the mists of night broke in the weak light of dawn, Chiksika sat on his horse at the forefront of the lines of warriors and gave the signal to charge. At his side was Tecumseh, who had vowed to protect his brother if at all possible.

The first wave of warriors descended on the fort. As they passed, they hurled burning brands of wood over the wooden stockade. The next wave rushed past firing arrows at the soldiers as they ran from the fires. Chiksika and Tecumseh led this rush, both crying out in frenzy and sending arrows whirring with deadly force at the uniformed soldiers.

They had made their first pass and turned to rush again when Tecumseh heard a terrible, soft crunching sound at his side. Chiksika was on the ground. A musket ball had smashed into his chest. The ball had cracked through a rib and the hole was right over the heart. Chiksika's eyes fluttered open as his brother held him. Tecumseh didn't speak, but put his arms under his brother and carried him from the field. He didn't even notice how effortlessly he had scooped up this man whom he had once imagined as the strongest and most powerful person in the world.

When he had laid him down behind a tree, he was surprised to hear Chiksika whispering something. "Do not bury me," were his words. "I have lived on the earth, not under it. I have never liked the idea of burial. Instead, my brother, set me on some hilltop, where the birds of the air can pick my bones. Will you promise me this?"

Tecumseh nodded. He closed his eyes as he fought back tears. When he opened them, the eyes that looked into his were glassy like the beads the Shawnee liked to bargain for from the white traders. Chiksika was dead.

Tecumseh took his brother's death very hard. He was hundreds of miles away from home, and the man who had raised him from a boy into a man, who had trained him in the ways of war and whom he loved more than anyone else, was dead. For the first time in his life, Tecumseh felt alone. But he did not allow his anger and frustration over Chiksika's death to eat away at him. Instead, he determined to direct his energy at those who had killed Chiksika. The white men had killed his father, had split up his family, had broken down the traditional way of life of his people, and now they had killed his brother. As he placed his brother's body on a lonely hilltop, he promised to continue on the warpath against the Americans.

Tecumseh did not go home after Chiksika's death. He and his band of Shawnee and Cherokee warriors stayed in the southern region for two years, waging war on American forts and settlements. Swift, deadly Indian attacks became regular occurrences for the settlers of Tennessee, Mississippi, and Alabama. The settlers learned to fear a certain eerie, unnatural quiet that descended in the middle of the night or just before dawn, for it was often followed by blood-curdling shrieks, the blasts of musket-fire, and the horrifying glow of flames licking at their cabin walls.

In these raids, Tecumseh honed the skills of war Chiksika had taught him. He also practiced his military strategy, always changing tactics. He would attack from the river one night, from the treetops another. Sometimes he would have his braves send their burning arrows flying in silence and sit watching the buildings of a settlement burn while the settlers still slept, unaware of the terror that was upon them. Other times he would invade the settlement, chase the white folk out of it, and then burn it down at his leisure.

Tecumseh was only twenty years old when Chiksika died, but to all the warriors he was the obvious choice to succeed Chiksika. Just as others in the tribe had natural ability in the arts of painting or carving, Tecumseh had a natural talent for the art of war. With astonishing speed he could grasp the important facts of a situation and decide how to face it. He seemed to know how the white men thought and could guess what they would do in a situation. And most importantly, he had the ability to rouse his braves to combat with stirring, fiery speeches.

The Shawnee and Cherokee warriors would sit spellbound, like children listening to a storyteller, as Tecumseh explained to them the long train of evils the whites had committed against the Indians. He spoke powerfully, and his braves listened with eager faces. With each raid, their devotion to Tecumseh grew stronger.

As a leader Tecumseh made some mistakes, but, being a good student, he learned from them. With each succeeding attack his skills as a war leader improved. His two years in the South prepared Tecumseh for the business of his life: war.

᪥᪥᪥᪥᪥ **6** ᪥᪥᪥᪥᪥

The Lesson of Pontiac

I
n 1790, as chilly November winds warned of
the return of winter to the Ohio River Valley,
Tecumseh led his party of devoted, war-trained
Shawnee braves over familiar grassy headlands.
After two years in the South, they were home again.

Tecumseh greeted his sister Tecumpease joyfully.
She had aged considerably in two years, but she
looked well. Tecumpease now had a husband and
children of her own as well as her two young
brothers to look after. She and many other women
in the village wept at the news that Chiksika had
died. But she was grateful that at least one of the
brothers had returned.

As the entire village sat around a communal fire
that night, Tecumseh and his braves took turns
telling of their adventures in the South and of their

many successes and their hopes that the whites would eventually give up their plans to expand westward. Then Tecumseh and his braves heard about what had gone on in Ohio while they had been away. The warriors who had stayed behind had not been idle. Tecumseh listened intently. He was pleased to hear that, besides the Shawnee, there were many other tribes in the North who refused to allow the whites to go unpunished. The Miami and the Kickapoo—whose villages were scattered throughout Indiana and Ohio—had been active along with the Shawnee, and great battles had been fought.

Tecumseh learned that the year before the Americans had established a fortress called Fort Washington on the Ohio River in the middle of the Shawnees' lush hunting territory. Immediately, white settlers had begun moving in. It was said that the Americans were planning to build a city on this spot, which they would call Cincinnati. Arthur St. Clair, governor of the Northwest Territory, had sent 1,500 troops from the fort to stamp out Indian resistance in the area.

This fearsome force had sped northward to attack Miami Indian villages. The pounding of 3,000 marching feet echoed like thunder through the forests. But a surprise awaited the troops. Before they reached the Miami lands, they walked into an ambush set by Shawnee, Miami, Delaware, and Ottawa Indians, who had been provided with muskets and ammunition by the British. Fierce fighting followed, and when the smoke had cleared nearly 200 American soldiers lay dead. It was a complete victory for the Indians. Warriors who had fought in the battle proudly led Tecumseh and the others into their wigwams to show them the white scalps—souvenirs from the battle hanging beside deerskin paintings and beadwork panels that the women made.

Tecumseh tingled with pride upon hearing of the cunning and bravery of the Shawnee warriors. He was pleased that other northern tribes were taking the threat from the Americans seriously. He hoped soon to get a chance to fight alongside them.

* * *

The following autumn, Tecumseh got his chance. Governor St. Clair had suffered much embarrassment when news of the ambush reached President Washington. He was determined to lead a massive expedition against the Indians. He hastily gathered more than 2,000 men from all parts of the territory, equipped them with a ramshackled assortment of firearms and artillery, and provided hulking supply wagons to accompany them.

In September this mighty force set out from Fort Washington in search of Indians. St. Clair was prepared to march his troops many miles. He was certain that they would find and destroy the most troublesome of the territory's Indians. What he didn't know was that the Indians knew about the march. It would have been impossible for the Indians not to notice the assembling of such a large and noisy force.

By the time the troops departed, the Indians were ready for them. As the groaning wheels of the cannons and supply wagons squeaked past the gate of Fort Washington, Tecumseh watched from high up in the wooded hills. He was acting as scout for the tribes in the area. Like a shadow, he and his small band of loyal Shawnee warriors followed the cumbersome army. Sometimes they swung around and traveled several miles ahead of the army, making a game of backtracking through the dense woods to relocate them. Every time St. Clair shifted his course, Tecumseh sent a messenger off to nearby villages to alert them. As the Americans marched through abandoned village after abandoned village, they grew more confused and frustrated.

Eight weeks after the army had set out, a full attack force of Indians—including Kickapoo, Miami, Delaware, Ottawa, and several hundred Shawnee—had assembled in northern Ohio to meet it. But word came from Tecumseh that the ponderous army would not reach their position for many days, so the eager Indian war party set off southward to meet the enemy.

They caught up with Tecumseh at his scouting post just north of the army's camp on the Wabash River. There the chiefs held numerous discussions about how to attack. At one point it seemed that all would be lost. The Miami and the Delaware chiefs had different strategies and each believed his was the

Waiting for soldiers

only way to victory. Young Tecumseh settled the argument by suggesting a third and very simple strategy. There was no need for complicated plans, he said, for the American army was so stupid that all the Indians had to do was surround them and pour gunshot into their camp.

The chiefs all agreed to follow the advice of the man who had been scouting the army. On the rainy, cold night of November 3, the Indians fanned out in a wide circle around the army's camp. The braves lay on the sodden ground and waited. After what seemed like hours, the noisy camp at last grew silent. The only sound was that of the steady patter of rain on the leaves.

Then the braves heard a whistling, cricketlike sound. It was repeated at intervals and soon had swept around the whole wide circle. At this signal, the warriors crept to their feet and moved in closer to within sight of the wagons and tents.

Again there was a long wait. Tecumseh's sharp eyes stayed focused on the tents. He began to hear movement. He lifted his hand skyward and looked at it. The dark sky glowed around it, telling him that dawn was nearing. The troops were waking.

A moment later there was a whooping whistle. Following the signal, Tecumseh raised his musket and took aim. This was a moment he loved, the instant just before battle. Now the world was silent and at peace. In two seconds, the great booming and shrieking of battle would rip through the silence.

As if they all had had stopwatches, the entire Indian army opened fire at the same instant. Hundreds of explosions rocked the forest. Birds squawked in panic. The sound of the rainfall was drowned out. In the next instant cries echoed from the camp. Tecumseh could pick out their English words: "Alarm!" "Indians!" "To arms!" Smiling at their panic, he reloaded, took aim, and squeezed his trigger again.

The battle lasted three hours and the Indians were never in danger. Even as the light increased, the soldiers were unable to locate their enemies. They hid as best they could behind their wagons and shot at tufts of grass, hoping for a hit.

The weak light of a gray morning still covered the scene when the deafening sound of musket-fire stopped. For a moment the silence returned. In the center of the Indians' deadly circle, 650 American soldiers lay dead. The rest had managed to create a breach in the Indians' southern flank and escape.

Soon the silence was broken by a cheer that swept around the circle and moved into the center of the ruined camp as the warriors left their positions. They began ripping open crates of supplies and dividing them among themselves. The chiefs gathered and complimented one another's warriors in the formal language of warfare. It was a great victory. To many of the chiefs, it proved that the Indians were stronger than the forces of the fledgling nation.

Tecumseh, standing among them, was as pleased as the rest, for he had just learned another lesson of vital importance. He now believed that it was possible for the Indians to defeat the Americans once and for all, and to drive them back across the Appalachians. But no tribe could do it alone. To accomplish this task, the Indians would have to unite into one great nation.

Tecumseh had learned the lesson of Pontiac.

7
Fallen Timbers

Tecumseh was feeling very good. When news of the defeat of St. Clair's army reached the East, the flow of white settlers into western lands stopped almost completely. Also, the victory had given him and his followers a burst of confidence.

With a hopeful heart, Tecumseh set off again with his growing band of young warriors for southern lands. The successful union of many different Indian tribes in the victory against Governor St. Clair had planted the idea of a great Indian alliance in Tecumseh's mind. He wanted to ride among the tribes of the South and spread the word that there was strength in unity.

For nearly two years the warriors traveled, sometimes aiding local tribes in attacks on white military posts and settlements. But Tecumseh's main purpose was to talk about unity. In many villages, including some Shawnee villages that were scattered through Alabama and Georgia, he received a cool reception. A union with all tribes was a new idea to most Indians and difficult to accept. Many of the tribes were enemies, and the chiefs couldn't imagine anything sillier than joining forces with their rivals. How dare this brash young warrior come into their villages and tell them how to run their affairs?

Tecumseh talks of tribal unity

But some tribes did listen. Creek, Cherokee, and Shawnee villages throughout the South had had their share of white settlers grabbing land and killing animals. Many young braves were fed up. They eagerly joined the band of ardent warriors led by this young, brilliant chief.

Pleased with his success, Tecumseh and his followers headed back North. On their way home, however, they were attacked while they slept by a band of Kentucky settlers led by Simon

Kenton, a rugged frontiersman widely known as a fearless Indian fighter.

Tecumseh was jolted out of his sleep by the echoing boom of rifle blasts. In one swift move he rolled to his feet and leaped behind a stump for protection, his musket in his hands. It was dark, but the Long Knives were not nearly so good at hiding themselves as Indians were, and Tecumseh could see that there were hundreds of them among the trees circling the camp. The settlers fired on the Indians eagerly. The braves were easy targets; they scrambled madly in the confusion, hunting for a hiding place and leaving their guns behind.

Suddenly, a deep, resonating voice boomed orders at them. Instantly, the warriors seemed to come to their senses. They listened. Tecumseh had quickly assessed the situation and was barking a complicated series of commands. The whites hopelessly outnumbered the braves and were in a better position. There was no choice but to escape. Then a thought flickered in Tecumseh's mind. He smiled. Would it work?

He called out more orders. Following his lead, the braves dropped to the ground and scrambled as fast as they could out beyond the rim of white men. By acting together most of them managed to get free. Once outside, instead of having them turn on the enemy, Tecumseh ordered his men to rush to where they could hear the enemy's horses stamping. Meeting there, they swiftly mounted the horses and dashed off, leaving Simon Kenton and his men helpless and on foot in the midst of the forest. Once again, Tecumseh had outwitted his enemy.

Upon reaching home, Tecumseh learned that once again the United States Army was on the move against them. A general named Anthony Wayne was leading an army of over 3,000 soldiers through Ohio. At strategic spots they stopped to

construct forts. General Wayne's mission was to negotiate treaties with the Indians. But the two powerful old Shawnee chiefs—
Blue Jacket and Black Hoof—knew that with thousands of
armed soldiers behind the general there would be no negotia-
tion. If the Indians voiced any objections, they would be
silenced with guns.

These older chiefs were more cautious than Tecumseh in
dealing with the Long Knives. But even they saw that their only
recourse was to fight. They quickly assembled as many braves
as they could, but the total number came to only about 1,400.
Against a better-armed force of more than 3,000 they wouldn't
stand a chance. The Indians hoped that by choosing the place
and time of the battle they would have the advantage.

The place they chose was a clearing along the Maumee
River in northern Ohio. The Indians entered the clearing at
dusk. Just a few months before it had been a dense forest. But
a whirling tornado had whipped across the land, ripping mighty
trees from their roots and sending them crashing to the ground.
Now the Indians stepped gingerly into an open, scarred field.
They looked at the devastation in awe. Tecumseh pointed to the
twisted trunks at their feet and reminded his warriors that
the Great Spirit was mightier than all humankind. The petty
wars between whites and Indians were nothing beside the
power of the Great Spirit, he told them. The Indians sat in the
clearing, wondering at the forces of nature and waiting for
the American army.

But before the army arrived a terrible storm swept in,
lashing the trees and swelling the river. Many of the Indians,
quaking in fear, took this as a sign that the Great Spirit was
displeased with them. Perhaps he was about to send another
tornado! Tecumseh kept his warriors at his side, but many

followers of Black Hoof and Blue Jacket fled in a panic. When the dawn light showed the approaching army of white soldiers, only 400 Indians remained to face them.

Quickly, Tecumseh summoned his warriors to him. As always, no matter what the odds they were ready to fight with him. They ran ahead of the advancing army, skipping nimbly over fallen logs. They hid themselves in the brush along the road and sat listening to the horses' hooves and the beating of their own hearts.

Suddenly, an advance party rounded the bend, heading at a full gallop toward the battle site. From the Indians' position on the ground, the soldiers on their massive steeds seemed impossibly tall and invincible.

Then Tecumseh gave a cry and his men opened fire. Instantly, a dozen soldiers dropped. Those behind halted their gallop. Horses winnied and reared in panic. The Indians fired again, but by now the soldiers had joined with the main body and, in a deafening rush, the whole force thundered down the path, past the Indians, and into the clearing.

Tecumseh's warriors followed the troops. The other Shawnee, waiting in the clearing behind fallen logs, opened fire. But the terrifying army was far too powerful to be stopped by so small a force. General Wayne shouted orders and companies of soldiers set off in different directions. Within moments, the Indians were surrounded. Tecumseh and his band fought valiantly, but within a short while most of the Indians had either fled or been killed. Tecumseh realized that they had to escape, but the situation looked impossible since they were surrounded and their horses had been killed.

Tecumseh thought back to the battle against Simon Kenton's frontiersmen. He decided to use the same tactic. Following his orders, his warriors charged one group of mounted soldiers on the perimeter of the fighting. Firing as they went, the Indians killed many of them. At close range they took out their tomahawks and hacked into the soldiers. Within a few seconds, they were mounted on the soldiers' horses and fleeing into the forest. They had escaped.

The Battle of Fallen Timbers, as it came to be known, was a devastating defeat for the Shawnee. Hundreds of their best warriors were killed. What was worse was that their confidence in their ability to defeat the white men had completely disappeared.

A few nights later the chiefs gathered to discuss the situation. Black Hoof and Blue Jacket shook their heads in dismay. They each spoke to the assembled Shawnee, and each said the same thing: The battle had proved that the white men were stronger than the Indians. The best hope for the Indians was to come to an agreement with the Americans. They would ask for fair treaties.

On August 3, 1795, chiefs from the Shawnee and several other Indian tribes met with General Wayne at the little town of Greenville, Ohio. There the Indians signed a treaty. For some supplies, worth about thirty thousand dollars, they agreed to sell most of what is today the state of Ohio, a chunk of Indiana, and large sections of what are now Illinois and Michigan. Land where for centuries Indians had been born, lived, and died suddenly belonged to someone else. Blue Jacket and Black Hoof were not happy to do this, but they believed there was no choice. Besides, the white men now guaranteed that the remaining lands would be Indian lands forever.

But when the chiefs and warriors from the assembled tribes had met before signing the treaty, a young chief named Tecumseh had stood up and, in a voice that rang through the trees, cried that he would have no part in their treaty. This shocked the chiefs. How dare this youngster refuse to follow his elders? But Tecumseh stood firm.

"This land belongs to me as well as to all Indians," he said. "These men," he went on, pointing his finger at Blue Jacket and Black Hoof, the Shawnee chiefs, "have no right to sell it. The sale is not proper. I will not honor it!"

All the chiefs were amazed and shocked. This young man was defying them! They looked at one another and tried to think of what to say, but before they knew what was happening Tecumseh had leapt onto a horse and sped away, dust flying behind him. What was more, several of the younger chiefs, who until now had followed the lead of their elders, left the council and hurried down the dirt road after Tecumseh.

A terrible blow had been struck to the Indian movement. Not only had they lost an important battle, but their chiefs, out of fear of the American army, had signed away most of their lands. But all was not lost. Those Indians who wanted to continue fighting the whites, and who did not agree with the old chiefs that the whites would leave them alone, now had a new leader to follow. In the months following the signing of the Treaty of Greenville, more and more passionate young warriors joined Tecumseh's party.

Tecumseh was now openly at odds with the older Shawnee chiefs. Indians throughout the territory became aware of a powerful new leader among the Shawnee: a chief who, instead of signing land away, swore to return the old lands to the Indians.

8
A Dying Tradition

Tecumseh had set his heart and mind to fighting for the Indian homeland and traditions. The Shawnee, like all their neighboring tribes, had lived on their lands for centuries and had developed traditions that made them proud. But steady contact with Europeans, especially with traders, had made them dependent on things that they could not make themselves. They liked the steel knives, the soft cloth, and especially the guns that the white men brought them. But these things had changed the ancient traditions and had weakened the Shawnee.

The Shawnee were part of an ancient race that had always lived with nature. For centuries before any white men came, they had survived and prospered, eating animals from the forests and fish from

Hunting was the Shawnee way of life

the rivers, using trees and animal skins to build their homes and to clothe themselves. They whittled bones into sharp, strong fishhooks, and made knives and arrowheads from flint—a hard substance that could be notched to razor sharpness.

The men were excellent hunters and brought home deer, elk, bear, and buffalo. Nothing was wasted from a hunt. The women dried much of the meat for later use. They also tanned the hides and fashioned them into clothing. Soft buckskin was used for fringed leggings and for dresses. Bearskins were made into coats for winter. Everyone wore soft, tough doeskin moccasins.

This way of life was very successful. A thousand years before Tecumseh's time the ancestors of the Shawnee were living in villages in the Ohio River Valley that were much the same as Tecumseh's village. The Shawnee persevered because they lived with the forest, not just in it. They understood their world. They were conservationists. For hundreds of years they and the forests lived together, and both prospered.

But their peaceful way of life was not to last. Thousands of miles to the east, across the vast ocean that the Indians called "the big lake," lived the Europeans. They had a different view of life. They were not content to live as their fathers had. They wanted a better life. They asked questions about the world around them, and slowly figured out ways to conquer it and to make it work for them. They invented telescopes, clocks, and guns, and built enormous ships that could sail for thousands of miles.

Three hundred years before Tecumseh was born, the European nations began a great race to conquer new lands. Their ships sailed to Africa, India, and the exotic Spice Islands of Southeast Asia.

In 1492, one of these adventurous seamen, Christopher Columbus, convinced the Spanish king and queen to let him sail west instead of east. Columbus believed that the Earth was round and that by going west he would reach the Spice Islands. As we all know, there was something blocking his way, something that no one in all of Europe or Asia knew about. It was a whole new world: the continents of North and South America. Overjoyed by Columbus's discovery, other European nations sent ships to the new world to claim parts of it for themselves. England and France claimed most of North America.

As the centuries wore on and the English and French expanded their settlements, they came into greater contact with the native Americans, including the Shawnee. At first the Shawnee welcomed these strange white men who wore beards. They invited them into their wigwams, taught them their language, and marveled at their curious customs. The British and French set up trade routes throughout much of the eastern half of what is now the United States and Canada. The Indians happily traded furs for the wondrous products of the Europeans.

But all was not well. Not long after the traders had established their routes, the Shawnee and other tribes were struck by a series of terrible illnesses—smallpox, measles, and influenza.

Thousands of Indians died, but no one understood why. No one knew that the illnesses had been brought to the Indians by the Europeans, whose bodies had built up some resistance to them. When the diseases were introduced to North America, whole Indian villages at a time were wiped out by them.

Disease was not the only thing the Europeans brought to the Indians. They also brought steel knives that could cut much better and last much longer than knives of stone or flint. They introduced the Shawnee to soft cloth and to metal pots that seemed to last forever. And they brought guns. With a musket, some gunpowder, and a few hard musket balls, an Indian hunter could shoot farther than with the best-made bow and arrow. Here, thought the warriors, was an amazing new weapon.

The problem with these new things was that in time the Shawnee came to look upon them as necessities. After a while, Shawnee women decided they couldn't cook without metal pots or skin deer without steel knives. Although the men still used bows and arrows, tomahawks, and clubs, they came to rely on the musket for hunting and protection. Since the Shawnee couldn't make any of these new things, they were at the mercy of the white traders.

As the Indians came to rely on these new products, their customs and way of life began to change. Women no longer taught their daughters how to make pots from bark and pitch. Men gave their sons more training with muskets than with Indian weapons. As a result, the Indians began to lose faith in their traditions. Perhaps, some began to think, the white man's culture really was better. Maybe they should give up their old ways altogether and live like white men. It was thinking like this that had led some chiefs to sign Indian lands away to the Americans. These chiefs had all but given up hope for a return to the old ways.

That was why, when a young Shawnee chief came storming into Indian villages, with strength and youth shining in him and the fire of righteousness glowing in his eyes, young warriors became excited.

* * *

Tecumseh rode throughout the territory to stir up opposition to the Treaty of Greenville. He worked tirelessly, with passionate devotion to his cause. Many of those who listened to his speeches around village campfires left with a fire burning in their hearts. They had been made to realize that their whole way of life was about to come to an end unless they fought to protect it. And here, they knew, was the chief to lead them.

When Tecumseh was not making the rounds of surrounding villages, he lived as a warrior. He loved to hunt with the men of his village, returning home with deer or elk meat slung over his horse's haunches. Though Tecumpease had a husband who provided the family with meat, Tecumseh's kills were an important contribution.

Powder-horn and pouch

The same sense of caring and decency that made Tecumseh forbid the torture of prisoners during war also made him sensitive to the needs of the unfortunate members of the tribe. There were many old men and women whose sons had been killed in battle or by disease. These people would starve if there was no one to hunt for them. Tecumseh knew who the neediest members of the tribe were, and he always made a point of looking in on them when he returned from his missions. When he hunted, he hunted for them as well as for his family.

Although he was devoted to his tribe and his family, Tecumseh had never been interested in starting a family of his own. He was now twenty-eight years old—an age at which most warriors had wives and children.

For a time after Tecumpease's marriage, Tecumseh continued living with her, her husband and children, and his two younger brothers. Tecumpease enjoyed having her favorite brother share her wigwam, but after a while she decided to have a talk with him. She explained to her brother that it was time he began raising a family. All able young men must do this, she said. It insured the future of the tribe. Her brother—now a tall, athletic young man with ribbons of muscle across his shoulders and back; deep, searching eyes; and an expressive face—smiled sheepishly. The problem, he told her, was that he never seemed to have time for such things. There was too much else to do. Besides, what woman would want a man who was never home to provide for her?

At last, at Tecumpease's insistence, Tecumseh married a woman named Manete. Everyone in the village thought this a strange match. Manete was older than he and men always married women who were much younger. But Tecumseh hadn't chosen because of love or beauty. He had picked hurriedly, considering marriage nothing more than a duty.

It wasn't long, though, before Manete began complaining about his long absences. When Tecumseh tried to reason with her, to explain the seriousness of the Indians' situation and of the urgent need for unity, she simply turned her back and refused to listen. He pointed to her metal cooking pots and knives, trying to make her see how dangerously dependent the Shawnee were on the white men. This situation must be changed, and he was the one to do it.

Manete could not understand this talk. It was all too remote for her. Tecumseh's only other close relationship with a woman had been with his sister Tecumpease, who was intelligent and concerned. He soon realized that Manete was neither of these. She was simply a woman who expected her husband to provide meat, give her a family, and protect her. Besides, she didn't like how the other women were always talking about the way Tecumseh would restlessly roam the forests, going from village to village like a white fur trader. She didn't want a husband who was the talk of the village.

Manete gave birth to a son. But the birth weakened her, and not long afterwards she died. The boy, whom Tecumseh named Pachetha, was taken in by Tecumpease. As far as Tecumseh was concerned, this ended his attempts at becoming a family man. He had no great interest in love. War was his passion, and it was an all-consuming one.

In later years, however, long after Tecumseh's death, a legend grew among the white settlers of Ohio about a love affair between the Indian chief Tecumseh and a young woman named Rebecca Galloway. She was the daughter of John Galloway, who owned a farm near Old Piqua and had been a famed Indian fighter in his younger days. According to the story, Tecumseh first met Rebecca while visiting her father, now eager to keep good relations with the local Indian villages. Tecumseh had never before seen a woman with blond hair and he was thunderstruck.

The chief visited the Galloway home several times, and each time he and Rebecca became more friendly. Eventually, the Indian chief and the white woman took to sitting together on warm afternoons while Rebecca gave him English lessons. She then taught him to read English and the two would sit together on the front porch of the log cabin reading passages of Shakespeare's plays to one another. Rebecca gave him a book on world history. Of all the figures he read about, Tecumseh most admired Alexander the Great, who had conquered the ancient world and forged a great kingdom.

According to this legend, Tecumseh asked Rebecca to marry him and she accepted. However, she told him that if they were to marry he would have to give up his traditional ways and live as a white man. Hearing these words come from her mouth woke Tecumseh from his romantic daydream. She couldn't possibly understand him if she didn't know that his whole life was devoted to driving the Long Knives from Indian lands! He, Tecumseh, live as a white man? Ridiculous! Tecumseh left the Galloway house, never to return.

If the story of Tecumseh and Rebecca Galloway is true, it marks the one and only time Tecumseh let himself be sidetracked from his mission in life. Never again would that happen.

9

The Rise of the Prophet

Tecumseh's brother, Lalawethika—the "Noise Maker" who had caused so much trouble as a boy—had grown into a lazy, good-for-nothing man. He had a wife and children, but he was usually too drunk on whiskey bought from the white men to provide meat for his family. His wife was a patient woman, but she was always at her wit's end with Lalawethika.

All during his childhood Lalawethika had been a problem. His older brother Tecumseh was the model of an Indian boy—strong, brave, clever, and caring. Lalawethika couldn't hope to match any of Tecumseh's great achievements. Kumskaukau, the other surviving triplet, was a good child who joined in the games and learned the traditions of hunting and warfare with the other boys. He became a good warrior, but never a great one.

Lalawethika always seemed to have a chip on his shoulder. As a boy he never played fair, and when he and Kumskaukau were old enough to learn to hunt, he immediately disliked it. His aim often went wild, and he was so careless that more than once he came close to hitting a fellow hunter. When Chiksika would scold Lalawethika, he just sneered and turned away. Finally, Chiksika forbade Lalawethika to join the hunt.

This suited Lalawethika just fine. He preferred the easy life in the village to the rigors of traveling and hunting. He would spend his days lazing around the wigwam, eating and talking about himself to whoever would listen. He was constantly talking, chattering about how well he could hunt if he chose to devote any effort to it, and how intelligent he was. He was a great listener too. He became the village gossip and always seemed to know what was going on in each family's wigwam.

When he was a teenager, Lalawethika discovered whiskey. Soon he became a regular drinker and went around to the other boys boasting about how much he could drink. When he was drunk, he was even noisier and more insulting than usual. The whole village began to despise him.

Tecumpease became fed up with her little brother. She urged him to go out and practice his hunting. She genuinely wanted Lalawethika to improve his ability, but she also wanted him out of the way. He was a constant nuisance.

Occasionally, Lalawethika would follow his sister's advice. Picking up a bow and some arrows, he would set off into the forest in search of game. On one such outing he took some whiskey too. Finding no animals, he sat down and got drunk, and then started wandering. Soon he was lost and darkness was approaching. He sat down and held his head in his hands, feeling sorry for himself and wondering if he would ever manage to become a hunter who could provide for a family.

Suddenly, a turkey squawked a few yards in front of him, and Lalawethika jumped to his feet. Confused by drink and excitement, he fitted his arrow onto the bowstring, raised it, and shot. In his confusion, though, he had turned the bow backwards, so that the arrow flew right into his eye.

From then on Lalawethika wore a patch over his empty right eye socket. He gave up hunting altogether, since it proved especially difficult with only one eye.

Lalawethika did manage to find a wife when the time came. His wife cared for him diligently and did all the chores. But at the age of thirty, he was still unable to fulfill the husband's role of bringing home the game that would supply meat and skins.

While virtually the whole village loathed Lalawethika, his brother Tecumseh stood by him and took care of him and his family. He regularly brought deer and elk to Lalawethika's wigwam, and he never gave up hope that his brother would outgrow his lazy, immature ways. Tecumseh believed that Lalawethika's problems were not entirely his own fault. His drinking was indirectly the fault of the white men, who had introduced whiskey to the villages. The gloom and feelings of inferiority that plagued Lalawethika were becoming more common among members of various Indian tribes, as they steadily lost their lands and traditions.

About this time, when the Indians were feeling beaten and their pride was at its lowest point, a new force sprang up among them: religion. Several tribes throughout Ohio, Indiana, and the Old Northwest were becoming more religious. They looked to the Great Spirit to help them out of their troubles. This was not unusual. Many times in history, people who have been in very bad circumstances and see no way out have turned to religion for strength. Lalawethika, however, merely scoffed. He just drank more and grew more depressed and helpless.

Then one day when Lalawethika was sitting in his wigwam drinking whiskey and feeling sorry for himself, he tumbled over and fell face down on the ground. His wife entered the wigwam a while later and found him lying in this position. She screamed and Tecumseh and Tecumpease came running. The village medicine man examined Lalawethika, and, hearing no heartbeat, he pronounced Lalawethika dead.

Lalawethika's wife, though she was in shock, began discussing what had to be done for his funeral and burial. Tecumseh, Tecumpease, and Kumskaukau grieved over Lalawethika's death and comforted his wife.

Then, several hours after his collapse, Lalawethika opened his eye. His wife, who had been staring tearfully at him, screamed and ran outside. Tecumseh came running. There, sure enough, was Lalawethika sitting up and looking rather groggy.

The news of Lalawethika's death had just spread through the village. Now came the news that he was alive again! Villagers crowded around the wigwam entrance, eager for a peek. Then Lalawethika emerged from the wigwam. He stood straighter than he ever had before and wore such an unusual expression that he looked like a stranger. He strode outside, stood on top of a log seat, and addressed the astonished crowd.

"I have died . . . and come to life again!" he cried. The Indians gasped. "I have met the Great Spirit himself," Lalawethika went on, "and he has told me of his plan for the red men. Follow me, and I will lead you down the correct path. You have called me Lalawethika. From now on I am the Prophet bringing the message of the Great Spirit. From this day I shall be called Tenskwatawa."

Tenskwatawa meant "the Prophet" in Shawnee. At the moment of his reawakening Lalawethika's life was over and Tenskwatawa's life began. Tecumseh's brother had become the Prophet.

Immediately, the Prophet began preaching to the Indians. His "return from the dead" seemed like a miracle to the Shawnee. Those Indians who had grown up making fun of Lalawethika now looked upon the Prophet as a kind of saint. They listened to his words, and they obeyed his teaching.

The Prophet told his audiences of his view of heaven. Heaven, he said, was exactly like the choicest and richest forests and farmlands in their territory. The only difference was that in heaven there was no hardship, no severe winters, no fighting or arguing, and no white men.

Tenskwatawa - the Prophet

But, the Prophet warned, only those Indians who had proved themselves worthy could get into heaven. To be worthy, an Indian must live an honorable life. He or she must not drink alcohol and must not fight with family members or fellow villagers. Families who were more fortunate should help those who needed skins and food. And most important, Indians must not do business with the Long Knives. The whites were at the root of all the evil that had befallen the Indians. The goods they traded were slowly wearing away the Indians' traditions. The whiskey they sold made Indians stupid. And, worst of all, the land-hungry white devils were intent on pushing the Indians back farther and farther until they would one day fall into the ocean. The Long Knives, preached the Prophet, must be opposed at all costs.

This sudden change in the once lazy and drunken young man was so astounding that people believed he really had been dead and reborn. It was a different person who now addressed them. Soon Indians from surrounding villages heard about the Prophet, and they flocked to hear him. Here, they told one another, was a man who spoke truly about what the Great Spirit wanted Indians to do. The Great Spirit was calling them to rise up and fight the Americans!

* * *

Not everyone was completely thrilled with the Prophet's words. One man, William Henry Harrison, found them down-right disgusting. Harrison, a tall, bony-faced man with deep-set eyes, was governor of the Indiana Territory. He knew nothing yet of the war chief Tecumseh, but he had heard rumors about a great religious leader who had risen among the Indians and who was winning thousands of converts with his talk about returning to traditional values and overthrowing the Americans.

Harrison was a firm believer in America's right to conquer the West. Like many of his countrymen, he envisioned a time when the United States of America would stretch all the way across the enormous continent. One obstacle to this expansion was the Indians. Harrison knew that a man like this Prophet, who combined religion with politics, could be dangerous. He could rouse his followers to war on settlements and make American pioneers think twice about venturing into the new lands. Harrison had to think of a way to show the Indians that the Prophet was a phony. He wrote to several chiefs and asked them to test the Prophet to see whether he really was the messenger of the Great Spirit. Early in April of 1806 he wrote:

> *Demand of him some proofs at least of his being the messenger of the Deity. If God has employed him, he has doubtless authorized him to perform some miracles, that he may be known and received as a prophet. If he is really a prophet, ask of him to cause the sun to stand still, the moon to alter its course, or the dead to rise from their graves. If he does these things, you may then believe that he has been sent by God.*

Governor Harrison smiled to himself after sending this letter, thinking he had succeeded in raising doubts among the Indians about their prophet. Surely, he had nipped this problem in the bud.

But Harrison was mistaken. He had set the stage for the Prophet to become recognized by nearly all Indians in eastern America as the messenger of the Great Spirit. When the tribal chiefs began to express doubts and ask the Prophet for proof that he was who he said, he sent word to them, and to all Indians, that they should assemble at a certain place on the morning of April 16. Then, he calmly told them, he would make the sun stand still, just as Governor Harrison had suggested.

This, of course, was an incredible proclamation. On the appointed day, thousands of Indians descended on the village, all eager to see if the Prophet had the power to stop the sun. Many of them were already his followers, but even they could not quite believe that he had such power.

Shortly before noon the Prophet emerged. He was a huge and awesome figure wrapped in an earth-red cape. Two white feathers hung from the knot in his hair, and a white scarf covered his empty eye socket. A silver ring was through his nose.

The multitude hushed. The Prophet climbed on a high stump, raised his hands over the crowd, and then held them out to the sun, as if he were waiting for the sun to fall into them.

—*The Prophet stops the sun*

At first nothing seemed to happen. But over the next few minutes, a shudder swept through the Indians as they noticed that darkness was falling. Three minutes after the Prophet had beckoned to the sun, it had vanished entirely and the astonished crowd was standing in darkness!

Then the Prophet's voice boomed for the first time over the heads of the assembly. "Do not fear!" he cried. "It will return

64

now!" Slowly, the light grew stronger, until once again the crowd was bathed in springtime light.

Had the Prophet performed a miracle? Well, no. In fact, he had somehow learned from white men in the region that there was to be an eclipse of the sun on that day, and at exactly that time. For a short while, the moon would pass directly between the sun and the Earth and would block out the sun's rays. It would seem like night.

The Indians who had gathered to watch the Prophet had no scientific explanation of eclipses, however. For them, this was proof positive that the Prophet was indeed a messenger who bore the words of the Great Spirit.

So it was that Governor Harrison, in seeking to discredit the Prophet, instead had given him the opportunity to expand his power. Over the next few years his power continued to grow as Indians as far south as Florida and as far north as Canada heard of the amazing feats of the Shawnee Prophet. Tenskwatawa began to travel, moving from village to village and preaching a return to traditional ways and opposition to the whites.

The stage was now set for a great alliance of Indian tribes. The Shawnee had produced a great war chief to lead them in battle against the Americans, and now a great prophet to lead them back to their old ways.

10

The Warrior Politician

In the years following the disastrous Treaty of Greenville, Tecumseh did not go on the warpath. Instead he worked silently in the background, urging Indians to unite against the whites. He split permanently from the conciliatory leadership of Black Hoof, and took the eager, militant warriors with him.

Tecumseh never went along with the old chiefs' decision to give up Indian lands in Ohio in the Treaty of Greenville, but now he had to accept the reality of it. By now, tens of thousands of American settlers had moved into the Ohio region and were farming where he had grown up. Soon there would be enough people for the area to become a state. Tecumseh had no choice but to move farther west and set up a base there. He moved his band of war-eager followers from his village of Old Piqua on the Mad River into Indiana. According to the hated treaty, that land still belonged to the Indians.

From this base, Tecumseh rallied his steadily swelling army of braves and kept them fit and eager for battle. He was now a strong man of thirty, with flowing black hair and a hard-set, determined face. He was an exacting leader who kept his warriors unusually well disciplined. They followed a regular daily routine and reported to sub-chiefs. But Tecumseh wasn't always a gruff military chief. He also could be friendly, and even playful. He eagerly joined in when braves held wrestling contests. At night, he liked to tell jokes around the fire. As a leader, he was both hard and fair, and his men were passionately devoted to him.

In 1805, Tecumseh's brother had his religious awakening, and the following year the Prophet moved from Old Piqua to a new village at Greenville, Ohio. Tecumseh decided to move there as well and work with his brother. They were each driven by desire, and though their desires sprang from different sources—the Prophet's was religious, while Tecumseh's was political—both had the same end in sight: defeat of the Americans.

The Prophet had by this time become a powerful force among many tribes, and his commandments were faithfully carried out. He had often preached against allowing the customs of the white men to enter Indian life. He now focused on the white men's religion. Many Indians, through their contacts with missionaries and settlers, had become Christians. The Prophet taught that this was a grave wickedness and that the Christian religion would become a force that would split the Indian tribes. It must be eradicated.

The followers of the Prophet listened to his words and became caught up in them. Like a fire these religious zealots swept among the tribes in Indiana, seeking out Christians among the Delaware, Kickapoo, and Wyandot tribes and mercilessly slaughtering them. They refused to listen to sensible talk or protests but instead insisted on carrying out their extermination.

Tecumseh soon heard about these crimes and moved to put a stop to them. The last thing he would tolerate was Indians killing one another. He sent his warriors out among the tribes to tell them that the Prophet did not want his followers to destroy any Indian people. Eventually, the killings were stopped, but hundreds of Christian Indians had died.

Tecumseh thought long and hard about the killings. While he believed it was wrong for Indians to kill one another, he was relieved to have the Christian Indians out of the way because these Indians usually had the closest ties with the Long Knives. The Prophet's followers had been far too extreme, but, thought Tecumseh, they had the right idea.

Tecumseh then sent his warriors back to their home villages. Under his orders, they carefully worked to bring about changes in their own village leadership. Slowly, the chiefs who were willing to sell land or who had close ties to the American settlers were replaced by young, enthusiastic followers of Tecumseh, men sworn to the Indian cause.

Tecumseh had begun to think not only like a war chief, but also like a politician. He continued to travel from village to village gathering support for a great Indian alliance. Night after night he spoke before council fires to assemblies of Winnebago, Kickapoo, Wyandot, Miami, and Ottawa. By day he and his companions traveled through the lush, unspoiled forests of Illinois and Wisconsin. The feeling grew that he was preserving all this land for the peoples who were born on it.

In his speeches, Tecumseh made the Indians aware of the evil that the Americans were doing to them and he offered his alliance as a way to put an end to it. Hundreds of braves agreed to join him. Tecumseh told most of them to remain with their tribes and await his orders. One, however, a chief from the Sac and Fox Indians of Wisconsin, was so drawn by Tecumseh's zeal and vision that he insisted on following him. His name was Black Hawk, and he became Tecumseh's lieutenant.

When Tecumseh led his party back to Greenville, he hardly recognized the place. As the word spread about his Indian alliance and the Prophet's religious revival, Indians began pouring in daily to be a part of these great events. Hundreds of wigwams, built and decorated in the styles of a dozen different tribes, dotted the riverbank.

From his brother, Tecumseh learned that problems with the Americans were rapidly increasing. Not long after Tecumseh's return, an Indian agent from the U.S. government named William Wells sent a message to the village saying that he would like to meet with the leaders. The Prophet knew what this was about. Their village was located east of the boundary established in the last treaty, and so according to the Americans it was on United States land. The agent wanted the Indians to move.

The Indians assembled for the meeting, but to their disappointment Wells did not come. Instead he sent a messenger who read a letter telling the Indians that the United States government wished them to move. Upon reading the letter, the messenger stood in the middle of the circle of militant Indians, his legs shaking so hard his knees were knocking. He looked up at Tecumseh, waiting for a reply.

Tecumseh gave him a speech he would never forget. "This place," Tecumseh cried, waving his hands and striding forward into the center, "was given to us by the Great Spirit to light our fires in. The white man's government has no right to ask us to leave, and certainly it shall not force us to leave. The white man's government makes boundaries. We do not. The Great Spirit knows no boundaries, nor will his red people acknowledge any. Finally, tell your President Thomas Jefferson of the United States that we will not speak to William Wells, since he has not come as he promised. If President Jefferson wishes to speak to us again, he must send a man of note."

With that, Tecumseh gave a stiff wave and dismissed the man. It was not just a speech, it was a performance. He had shown his followers how a strong, proud Indian dealt with the Americans.

Tecumseh

Tecumseh's speech inflamed the Indians. The warriors from various tribes met separately and decided that they could not wait for the big war that Tecumseh promised. They wanted to act right away. Over the next few months, bands of warriors from Greenville occasionally dashed into the surrounding countryside and made their own little wars on settlements. Dozens of farmers and their families were killed by the raiders.

Now the governor of the new state of Ohio, Edward Tiffin, had to act. President Jefferson was eager for the nation to expand westward. For men and women to be willing to venture into the unknown lands they had to be convinced that they would be safe there. When reports of scalpings of settlers in Ohio reached Washington, D.C., Governor Tiffin was told that he must put a stop to the Indians. Tiffin then sent messengers to Greenville and other villages in the area, summoning all Indians to a great meeting. He wanted to determine who was responsible for these killings.

Tecumseh did not know who was behind the murders, but, seeing his old enemy Black Hoof at the meeting as the head of a group of weakling chiefs, he decided to use the meeting to his advantage. He delivered a long lecture to the American officials on the Indian view of land ownership. It seemed to the Americans that Tecumseh was ignoring the main topic and using the meeting for his own purposes.

Finally, one of the officials stood up and told the Shawnee leader that he was not addressing the issue. This was the opportunity Tecumseh had been waiting for. "We want to know one simple thing," said the man. "Who killed the settlers?"

Tecumseh smiled faintly and nodded as though he had only just now understood the purpose of the meeting. "Well," he said, walking over to Black Hoof and hugging him, "this is the man who killed your white brothers!"

At this, every man—American and Indian—leaped up screaming. Black Hoof's people were enraged. They called Tecumseh a wicked liar and challenged him to fight. Tecumseh's own people were crying out in astonishment. The Americans were shouting at one another as they tried to keep the two Indian camps separated.

The meeting ended, and the Americans learned nothing about the murders. To them it was a complete disaster. To Tecumseh, however, it was a grand success. He had used the meeting to widen the gulf between himself and Black Hoof. In doing so he had made his own militant position clearer to the Americans and to those of Black Hoof's warriors who might be having second thoughts about dealing with the Long Knives and who might someday want to join Tecumseh's party.

* * *

Two months later, Ohio had a new governor, a man named Thomas Kirker. Upset by the friction between the Indians and the settlers in his state, Governor Kirker called a second meeting to discuss the various problems. Chiefs from many tribes were present at this meeting, but one of these Indian leaders stood up and spoke so forcefully and clearly that it was as if he were the only speaker. Governor Kirker and the other American officials present learned that the Indian named Tecumseh was no ordinary chief, but a wiser and more clever leader than any they had ever seen, white or Indian.

Tecumseh's speech lasted for three hours. During those three hours, the Shawnee leader amazed the Americans by reciting in a cool, even voice the list of treaties that the white men had broken. First there was the British proclamation, which had promised the Indians that the settlers would remain east of the Appalachian Mountains. The settlers had broken that. Then the settlers warred on England and proclaimed their own nation. This new nation, in its thirty-year history, had repeatedly forced Indian tribes to sign treaties in which they gave up their lands but were guaranteed new, permanent homelands . . . only to have the government or settlers break the treaties a few years later.

The latest treaty, the Treaty of Greenville, was already being violated by settlers who were moving in great numbers into Indiana. How were the Indians to trust a government that made false promises? To whom could they turn with complaints when treaties were broken? They could only turn to their weapons.

Tecumseh assured the officials that the Indians would not make war on the United States. But neither would they permit any more lands to be ceded by tribal chiefs for, Tecumseh declared, no chief, no Indian, had the right to sell lands since Indian land belonged to all Indians, not to separate tribes.

With Tecumseh's great statement of land ownership he became not only a war chief, but a lawmaker too. From now on, he declared, he would not honor any treaty in which Indians gave up land to the whites. Indians, he had decided, did not have the same understanding of ownership as did white men. All Indian land belonged to all Indians. That meant that no group of Indians had the right to sell land. This statement was to become Tecumseh's guiding principle in his future dealings with the white men.

꧁꧁꧁꧁꧁ **11** ꧁꧁꧁꧁꧁

Distant Thunder

F our hundred miles away, another great leader also had been thinking about land. Thomas Jefferson was the new nation's third president. He had come into office campaigning for peace, and during his term the country had been at peace with all nations—except the Indian nations.

Jefferson was the drafter of the colonies' Declaration of Independence: that great document that declared the basic, inalienable rights of all people. All men, Jefferson had written, are entitled to life, liberty, and the pursuit of happiness. England had denied these basic rights to its colonists, and so the Americans broke away and formed their own nation. Now Jefferson was busy acquiring new lands so that the nation would grow and become more powerful. He had apparently forgotten that the Indians who lived in those lands were entitled to life, liberty, and the pursuit of happiness just as his countrymen were.

A few years earlier, in 1803, Jefferson had signed an agreement to buy from France one of the largest blocks of land ever sold. With a stroke of his pen, Jefferson added to his country the whole area from the Mississippi River to the Rocky Mountains. This area included the future states of Iowa, Missouri, Arkansas, Oklahoma, Kansas, Nebraska, South Dakota, Montana, and Wyoming, as well as parts of Louisiana, Minnesota, North Dakota, Colorado, and Texas.

Thomas Jefferson (by Gary Gianni)

When the French emperor Napoleon and President Jefferson made this deal, neither one thought to consult the dozens
of Indian tribes who lived on this land, and whose ancestors
had been born, lived, and died there. With the acquisition of
this land called the Louisiana Purchase, the United States had
doubled its size. It now stretched in an unbroken expanse from
the Atlantic Ocean to the Rocky Mountains. Compared to the
enormous country, the Indian tribes seemed ridiculously small
and no match for the might of the vigorous new nation.

Jefferson knew that some Indian chiefs in the lands just
across the Appalachian Mountains were resisting the settlers
coming into the region. In Ohio and Indiana especially, there
seemed to be mounting problems.

But now, near the end of Jefferson's second term in office,
he had other things on his mind. Sitting at a large, polished
oak table in the White House, he listened as James Madison,
his devoted secretary of state, outlined the recent difficulties
with England. England and France, the United States' two
largest trading partners, were at war and England had cut off
the United States' right to trade with either nation. This infuriated the Americans. What was more, many people in Washington, D. C., believed that the British were plotting to invade the
United States from their forts in Canada. Frowning, Jefferson
listened carefully as Madison told him that many American
officials were beginning to think the British generals in Canada
were urging the Indians in Ohio and Indiana, especially those
troublesome Shawnee, to make war on American settlements.

It was a tense time for the young nation. Some people were
even beginning to talk about a second war with England.

* * *

As it turned out, Madison's information was entirely wrong.
The American officials who thought the British were urging the

Indians to fight had their information backwards. It was the Indians, or, more precisely, one fiery Indian chief named Tecumseh, who were now gently prodding British officers in Canada to fight the Americans.

Tecumseh was very excited. He had journeyed to Fort Malden, a British stronghold in Canada on the shores of Lake Erie, to talk. He was a shrewd military leader. He had had long conversations with many British traders in Indiana, and from what they told him he could see that a war between England and America was coming. This was the chance he had been waiting for. He knew that even if all the Indian tribes united they would probably not be strong enough to defeat the Americans. But if they joined forces with the British, they would surely crush the American army and force the settlers to go back east, possibly back across the Appalachians. Everything depended on a meeting with Colonel William Claus, officer in charge of Fort Malden.

The two men met on a cool summer morning in 1808. Tecumseh was eager, but he had to be careful in his presentation. For one thing, he knew that all the white men believed his brother, the Prophet, to be the real leader of the Indian movement; and as far as the whites knew, it was strictly a religious movement. Tecumseh's mission was to show Colonel Claus that his business was not religion, but war.

The two men sat across a small table. Colonel Claus wore a full British military uniform. Tecumseh was dressed as usual in buckskin leggings and shirt, with a large white ostrich feather (acquired from a British trader) in his hair. He leaned on the table and his arm muscles bulged through the tight shirt. Colonel Claus was immediately impressed by the Indian's fervor.

Tecumseh began by sketching for the colonel his plan to link the tribes into a great Indian nation that would oppose the Americans. Tribes from Tennessee to Wisconsin would work together. Never before had the Indians cooperated on such a grand scale, but Tecumseh assured the colonel they would now.

Tecumseh then surprised Claus by telling him he believed Great Britain and America would soon be at war. It might be in one year, or two or three, but war was coming.

Then, abruptly, Tecumseh stopped talking. He didn't say anything about joining forces with the British. He waited for Claus to say it. He wanted the Englishman to ask him to join them.

Colonel Claus smiled. Here was no wild, unruly savage. This man Tecumseh, the Prophet's brother, was very, very shrewd. Just as Tecumseh had hoped, Claus then suggested that Great Britain join forces with the Indian alliance. He could see the wisdom in uniting with the Indians against the United States. Like Tecumseh, he wasn't sure when war would come, but he could already feel the distant thunder of cannons. It was best to be prepared.

The two men shook hands across the table. The Kingdom of Great Britain was now officially the partner of the united Indian nation.

12
Prophet Town

The Prophet strode through his village, frowning. What had once been a peaceful collection of wigwams nestled in a dense pine forest had grown into an ugly, dirty, overpopulated town. He walked through the little dirt alleys between the rows of wigwams, passing children and women who sat on the ground staring blankly into the sky or down at the earth. The Prophet's people were starving.

By 1808, Greenville had outgrown its fields. They could no longer supply the corn, beans, and melons necessary to feed the hundreds of mouths. The Indians had hunted the surrounding forests until not a single rabbit, turkey, or pheasant remained, much less deer or elk. The Prophet's followers were still devoted, but they were hungry. The Prophet winced in pain at the sight of so many people lying listless with hunger. Clearly, something had to be done.

At this time the Prophet received a visitor. His name was Main Poc and he was a medicine man from the Potawatomi tribe, which lived farther west in the Indiana Territory. Main Poc was the most famous and revered medicine man in his tribe. He had heard of the Prophet's teachings and had come himself to speak with him.

The two men immediately became friends. They both hated the whites, and they had very similar ideas of what the Great Spirit wanted the Indians to do. There was only one subject they disagreed on—whiskey. Main Poc was a big, burly Indian who drank huge quantities of whiskey every day. He said the Great Spirit had told him that whisky was the source of his power.

In spite of the fact that Main Poc was half-drunk most of the time, he and the Prophet got along well. After he had been at Greenville and had seen the poor condition the town was in, he offered the Prophet a section of the Potawatomi lands in Indiana on which to live. There, he said, the Prophet's people would have plenty of space to farm and hunt. It was good, rich land, and, best of all, there were no Long Knives for miles around.

The Prophet discussed Main Poc's offer with Tecumseh. The two brothers decided that this was a good plan and so, that same year, the entire village moved 150 miles west.

Tecumseh and his brother were thrilled with the new site. It was on the bank of the Wabash River, not far from its tributary, the Tippecanoe. It was surrounded by miles of green forests teeming with animals. On their way to their new home, the party had shot dozens of bucks, pheasants, grouse, and several bears, so they knew the forests were still rich hunting grounds. Here, the two brothers told one another, they would build a great town. It would become the center of a vast, strong, united Indian movement. The tribes would come together to fight the white men, and this spot would be the center of their great organization. This would be their capital city. They would call it Prophet Town.

The Prophet got to work directing his followers in construction of the new town. They spaced their wigwams neatly along the river, felled trees, and laid out plots for farming. Work went swiftly.

Tecumseh was not there to take part in the building of Prophet Town. He had returned to Ohio to make another swing through the villages of the Seneca and the Wyandot Indians that still hugged the rivers of his old hunting grounds. The time for action was edging closer. Now was the time to round up the young, eager braves and lead them to the new Indian capital. War lay ahead, and the Indian army had to be ready for it.

"Soon," Tecumseh said in village after village, "our day will come! Soon we will test the strength of the red men. You must prepare. When the day arrives, you must be ready to fight for your lands and your traditions!"

But, to Tecumseh's dismay, most of the Indians turned their backs on him. It was true that with so many white settlers moving in the Indians were unhappy in their lands, but the chiefs of the villages didn't like the idea of moving to a place where Tecumseh would take over the leadership of their people. Also, many Indians had grown suspicious of the Prophet's religion. They didn't want to move to Prophet Town, where they imagined the Prophet might cast strange spells on them.

Tecumseh was infuriated. He had never been interested in his brother's religion himself; he had simply joined forces with the Prophet because his religious movement matched so perfectly Tecumseh's dream of an Indian nation. The Prophet's

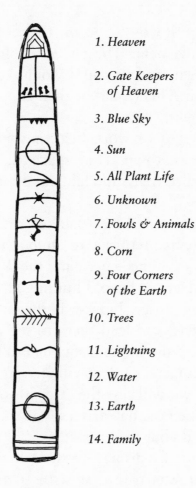

1. Heaven

2. Gate Keepers
   of Heaven

3. Blue Sky

4. Sun

5. All Plant Life

6. Unknown

7. Fowls & Animals

8. Corn

9. Four Corners
   of the Earth

10. Trees

11. Lightning

12. Water

13. Earth

14. Family

Shawnee prophet's sacred slab

religion had been convenient for Tecumseh. Now, however, it was starting to work against him.

* * *

The Prophet had learned from his brother that their movement could not be simply religious. Tecumseh had shown him that to drive the white men away from Indian lands, they would need more than just devout followers. They would need organization, weapons, and food. While Tecumseh was away struggling to get recruits, the Prophet decided to try his hand at politics.

His village had grown rapidly. Already the Indians had eaten most of the available food. The Prophet had to do something quickly. He decided to pay a visit to Governor William Henry Harrison, his old foe who three years before had so disastrously challenged him to make the sun stand still. He and several dozen of his followers made the journey to the territorial capital of Vincennes.

Harrison was surprised to see the holy man, and he was immediately suspicious, but he greeted him warmly. The Prophet was wrapped in a full-length robe and wore long, heavy metal earrings and a patch over his eye. He bowed to the governor and said how fine it was to meet the great man at last. The two leaders went inside the governor's mansion for their meeting.

"I want to show you that our religion is peaceful," the Prophet said. "That is why I have come." He then talked for a long while about his followers, the fine village they had built, and how they wished only to live in peace with the United States. Tenskwatawa was polite and humble before the governor. Never once did he reveal his true feelings or intentions.

Governor Harrison believed the story completely and was relieved to find that the terrible threat he thought the Indian movement presented did not exist. He eagerly offered to help the people of Prophet Town in any way he could. He insisted that the Prophet accept gifts of food and ammunition as signs of friendship. Solemnly, the Prophet accepted these.

Soon after, the Indian delegation left Vincennes. As they marched away, the Prophet smiled. He had lulled Harrison into believing there was no Indian threat, and he had gotten food and ammunition in the process. He had indeed learned a great deal from his brother Tecumseh.

The provisions from Governor Harrison did not last long. Several weeks later, when Tecumseh returned to Prophet Town with a heavy heart and only a few straggling followers, more troubles were there to greet him. While he had been away, Prophet Town had grown so vast so quickly that once again the fields and forests couldn't supply enough food for everyone. Nearly everyone was hungry, and a terrible epidemic of influenza had broken out. While this disease was usually not serious among white men, the Indians' bodies didn't have the antibodies to fight it. Many had died or were critically ill. Others who were not yet stricken decided to abandon the town while they were still able.

For a while after his visit to Governor Harrison, the Prophet had hoped all would be well. But the food shortage and the epidemic changed all that. Within a few weeks the influenza had done its worst and began to subside, but it left the Indians weak and dispirited. The town that the two brothers hoped would be the center of a great Indian alliance was in danger of collapse—just when the time for war was approaching.

Tecumseh, however, was not one to sit worrying and complaining. He was a man of action. Nothing would stop his Indian movement, not hunger or illness. Gathering a handful of his sturdiest and most trustworthy braves, he left Prophet Town once again. This time the Indian leader sped westward toward Illinois and the Mississippi River. As he had dozens of times now, he would ride among the tribes calling them to action.

The movement had weakened, but its leader was stronger than ever.

13
Tecumseh Turns the Tables

G overnor Harrison was furious. He was pacing back and forth in front of his office window. His white hair bristled and his deep-set eyes smoldered. Standing at the doorway at stiff attention were two lieutenants just back from a secret mission to Prophet Town. Their report had made the governor angry.

The Indians at Prophet Town, the lieutenants said, were preparing for war. They had amassed muskets and ammunition and were stockpiling food. Many of the Prophet's followers had abandoned the town following an outbreak of influenza, but many more remained. There was no question about it—the Shawnee Prophet's meeting with Governor Harrison had been one big lie.

"Curse him, that liar and scoundrel!" the governor cried, shaking his fist at the air. "That sneaking redskin fiend!" He was especially annoyed because he had recently sent a letter to his superiors in Washington, D.C., boasting that he had solved the Indian problem by befriending the Prophet, someone the white men still considered the overall leader of the Indian movement. Now President Jefferson would look on him, Harrison, as a complete fool. He had been duped by an Indian.

After Harrison's fury had cooled, though, a smile spread across his face as he thought of a plan to deal with the Indians and at the same time solve another large problem. The settlers in the territory of Indiana were pushing hard for statehood, and Governor Harrison, too, wanted very much for his territory to become one of the states of the Union. For Congress to approve this, however, the territory needed to have a population of at least 60,000. The problem was that every new settler would need a large tract of land to farm, but most of the territory's land had been declared offical Indian land by the Treaty of Greenville.

Governor Harrison's idea was to force the Indians to sign a new treaty that would grant the rest of their lands in the territory to the United States. With more land, more settlers could move in. Harrison thought it was a brilliant idea. And it would show that cursed Prophet that his Indian movement was no match for the United States of America.

Harrison went to work immediately on his plan. In the summer of 1809 he sent messengers to dozens of chiefs throughout the territory asking them to come to an important meeting. However, all the chiefs who assembled at Fort Wayne two months later were older men who had no fighting spirit. Harrison was clever. He did not bring out the treaty immediately. First he held a party, at which he provided as much whiskey as the Indians could drink. Once the chiefs were drunk, he showed them the paper and told them that, in exchange for their signatures, he would give them seven thousand dollars to divide among themselves.

Sacred Rattle

This sounded like a good deal to the drunken chiefs. Everyone signed. Governor Harrison had gotten the Indians to sign away most of their land in the territory. A fair court of law would almost certainly have declared this treaty, which became known as the Treaty of Fort Wayne, illegal. For one thing, the chiefs at the meeting did not represent all of the tribes in the territory and were in fact signing away lands that did not belong to them. But Harrison knew that no Indian was knowledgeable enough about the legal system of the United States to take the case to court.

Harrison was pleased with himself. He had added an enormous chunk of land to the United States; President Jefferson was pleased with him; and he had assured that his territory would soon become a state. Also, he was certain to become a state governor. Furthermore, Governor Harrison was sure that with this treaty he had dealt a deathblow to the so-called Indian movement.

* * *

When Tecumseh heard about the Treaty of Fort Wayne, he went wild with anger. Here he was, riding tirelessly through the forests of Illinois, up and down and even across the Mississippi River, and into far Missouri, talking at village after village until his voice was hoarse, trying to get Indians to halt the progress of the Americans—and behind his back a handful of chiefs calmly sign away a whole territory!

Tecumseh was usually an even-tempered man. His warriors had almost never seen him so angry. Now they were shocked at his reaction to the news of the treaty. He stormed, he raged, he shook his fists and swore. He threatened to kill every chief who had signed the treaty. What were the fools doing? Didn't they know they were giving up their land, their future, their traditions? And all for a few dollars' worth of supplies!

When Tecumseh calmed down, he headed back to Prophet Town. There he met with his brother and they discussed what was to be done. Still furious, Tecumseh sent word to Governor Harrison that to his mind the treaty was entirely illegal. He and his brother would not honor it. But already settlers were moving into the virgin forests that had belonged to Indians for generations. Trees were being felled, roads laid, and log fences cut across fields. Almost overnight the timeless, natural scenery was changing.

By now, Tecumseh had collected his wits. His fury was spent and his political shrewdness had returned. If he could foresee the disastrous results of the treaty—the hunting grounds turned into farms—then so must Indians all across the territory. Now, he thought, Indians would listen to him.

Once again he mounted his horse and, taking his trusted companions led by Black Hawk, sped off to deliver his message of Indian unity once again. It was wintertime, when Indians preferred the safety and warmth of their wigwams and campfires to the hardships and bitter cold of travel. But Tecumseh was certain that now was the time to act. He spoke as he always had, in bold, passionate words and phrases, accusing the Americans of stealing Indian land, and with it the Indians' past and future.

People who had ignored Tecumseh's speeches in the past now listened intently. Even among the villages whose chiefs had signed the treaty, people were having second thoughts. Suddenly, the white men were all around them, clearing land and bullying Indians—sometimes killing them. Everywhere Tecumseh went, people looked at him with pleading faces and asked him the same question: What was to be done?

Tecumseh was ready with his answer: Follow me!

And they did follow him. When the ice of winter melted and the first warm days announced the approach of spring, parties of warriors from the Sac and Fox tribes of Illinois arrived at Prophet Town. So did Delaware, Ottawa, and Miami. Old Main Poc rode into town, followed by a huge contingent of Potawatomi. The Prophet hadn't been in touch with Tecumseh, but he could see from the streams of Indians who came riding into Prophet Town that his brother had been successful in his mission.

As for Governor Harrison, once again a Shawnee had made a fool of him. This time, it was the Prophet's brother who had foiled Harrison. Tecumseh had used the signing of the Treaty of Fort Wayne, which Harrison had thought would destroy the Indian movement, to his own advantage. Harrison and other American officials now realized that the true leader of the Indian alliance was not the Prophet but his brother Tecumseh. They now saw that the ultimate purpose of the movement was not religion. It was war, terrible and final.

14

"Sell a Country! Why Not Sell the Air?"

E very day it seemed another tired and disheveled messenger reported to Governor Harrison that yet another band or tribe of Indians was in league with the Shawnee brothers. The Indian movement was growing by leaps and bounds.

Harrison was angry, but also frightened. He had never heard of Indians acting together in such a way. What kind of strength could they have if they all fought together? The governor shuddered to think of the mass slaughter of settlers throughout his territory that would surely come about if things continued as they were. He had to do something. He had to talk with the leaders of the movement, with the Prophet or this fellow Tecumseh. He decided to send a letter to explain the situation as he saw it and to invite them to a meeting. The letter had to be strong, if he was to convince the Indians of his power.

The governor sent a man named Baron to Prophet Town. Baron had delivered messages to the Indians before, but this trip to Prophet Town was a new experience for him. He was met by two young braves. They led him past dozens of wigwams, through winding lanes, along the riverbank, and then to an open-air pavilion. There in the center, the Prophet sat in his usual stunning dress—a full-length robe, feathers, earrings, and a nose ring. Stout warriors stood on both sides of him, their arms folded and their cold eyes looking straight ahead.

The Prophet stared at the messenger for several minutes without uttering a sound. Then his voice erupted. "For what purpose do you come here? Brouillette was here," the Prophet cried, naming an earlier messenger. "He was a spy. Dubois was here. He was a spy. Now you have come. You, too, are a spy!" The Prophet pointed to the ground just in front of Baron. "There is your grave!" he cried, his eye red with passion. "Look on it!"

Pictograph of medicine hunting song

By the end of this speech, Baron was quivering and was certain that he was about to be executed in some horrible way. Then he heard someone approaching. He turned and saw a tall and fine-looking Indian coming toward him. It was Tecumseh.

Tecumseh knew that the Prophet loved to act and work himself into a frenzy. He also knew that his brother had no intention of killing the man. Tecumseh told the messenger not to be afraid, promised that they would not harm him, and asked why he had come.

Baron, still shaken, composed himself and pulled the letter from his coat. He then read aloud:

> *William Henry Harrison, Governor and Commander-in-Chief of the Territory of Indiana, to the Shawnee chief and the Indians assembled at Tippecanoe:*
>
> *Notwithstanding the improper language which you have used towards me, I will endeavor to open your eyes to your true interests. There is yet but little harm done, which may be easily repaired. The chain of friendship which united the whites with the Indians may be renewed, and be as strong as ever.*
>
> *Don't deceive yourselves. Do not believe that all the nations of Indians united are able to resist the force of the Seventeen Fires [Governor Harrison meant the seventeen states]. I know your warriors are brave, but ours are not less so. But what can a few brave warriors do against the innumerable warriors of the Seventeen Fires? Our blue-coats are more numerous than you can count; our hunters are like the leaves of the forest, or the grains of sand on the Wabash. Do not think that the red-coats can protect you; they are not able to protect themselves.*

Governor Harrison finished by inviting the Indian leaders to meet with him at Vincennes. Tecumseh then told Baron that the Indians were indeed united, and that they would fight to the death unless the United States stopped pressuring Indians into signing away their lands. "The Great Spirit gave this great island to his red children, and he placed the whites on the other side of the big water," Tecumseh told Baron. "The Great Spirit ordered us to come here, and here we will stay."

Nevertheless, Tecumseh promised that he would come to Vincennes. Baron, thinking he was being gracious, said that the governor would allow Tecumseh to bring several of his braves

COURTESY MUSEUM OF THE AMERICAN INDIAN, HEYE FOUNDATION

Tenskwatawa - the Prophet

with him. Tecumseh frowned. He did not like being told what he could or could not do. He gruffly informed the messenger that he would bring as many warriors as he liked.

A month later, American lookouts in the fort just north of the town of Vincennes spotted an amazing sight on the Wabash River. About 400 Indians were paddling downriver in canoes, all of them splendidly dressed and painted. The commander later wrote: "The Shawnee Indians have come. They passed this garrison on Sunday last in eighty canoes. They were all painted in the most terrific manner. They were stopped at the garrison by me, for a short time. I examined their canoes, and found them well prepared for war in case of an attack."

The commander was especially impressed by the leader of the party. "They were headed by the brother of the Prophet, Tecumseh, who perhaps is one of the finest looking men I ever saw—about six feet high, straight, with large, fine features, and altogether a daring, bold looking fellow."

This enormous party of Indians camped just outside the town of Vincennes. Governor Harrison, who was distinctly annoyed at the number of braves Tecumseh had brought with him, invited the brother of the Prophet to meet at his home the next morning. Tecumseh agreed.

At the appointed hour, Tecumseh and a small party of warriors, including Black Hawk, stood in the bright sunlight before the governor's mansion. Governor Harrison stood in the courtyard to greet him. At his side were several army officers in full dress uniform and the judges of the Supreme Court of the Indiana Territory looking very dignified. Governor Harrison had invited the most important officials of Indiana. He was giving Tecumseh the honors of a high-ranking official. Also with him were two or three of the Indian chiefs who had signed the Treaty of Fort Wayne and were now friendly with the governor.

The two men greeted each other solemnly. Then Governor Harrison asked Tecumseh to come onto the porch, where he had chairs and tables arranged for their meeting. But Tecumseh shook his head. "Houses are built for you to hold councils in," he said. "Indians hold theirs in the open air."

The governor frowned. Already this Indian was being difficult. Nevertheless, he nodded and agreed to move the chairs onto the grass. Tecumseh told him only to bring chairs for the white men. "The earth is my mother," he said, "and on her bosom I will repose." He and his companions took their seats on the grass and waited for the meeting to begin.

Finally, all was ready. The two parties faced each other in the bright sunshine, the Americans seated on chairs and the Indians on the grass. American soldiers and Indian warriors were arranged in a large circle around them. The soldiers held muskets at their sides. The Indians were armed with bows and arrows, clubs, and muskets. Both sides kept their eyes on each other. Both were suspicious of a trap. A cool and refreshing breeze blew, but the atmosphere was tense.

Tecumseh spoke first. He knew how important this meeting was, and he was well prepared. If he could somehow convince Governor Harrison that the Indian movement was a reality, that the Indians were committed to fighting to preserve their lands, then the governor might take steps to ease tensions. In his heart, Tecumseh knew this was unlikely, but he was willing to try.

"Brother," he began, his eyes fixed on Harrison, "I wish you to listen to me well. Since the peace was made, you have killed some of the Shawnee, Winnebago, Delaware, and Miami, and you have taken our land from us. I do not see how we can remain at peace if you continue to do so. You want, by your distinctions of Indian tribes in allotting to each a particular tract of land, to make them go to war with each other. You never see an Indian come and endeavor to make the white people do this. You are continually driving the red people. At last, you will drive them into the Great Lake, where they will not be able to stand."

Governor Harrison stared firmly into Tecumseh's eyes as the Indian spoke. While the governor showed no emotion, he was astonished at the Indian's powerful presence and stunning intellect. He listened with fascination, as if listening to a great actor give a speech in a play.

"Brother," Tecumseh went on, "the lands that were sold and the goods that were given for it were done by only a few. The Treaty of Fort Wayne was made through threats. If the land is not restored to us, you will see, when we return to our homes, how it will be settled. We shall have a great council, at which all the tribes will be present. I am the head of all the tribes. I am also a warrior, and all the warriors will meet together in two or three moons from now. Then I will call for those chiefs who sold you the land, and I shall know what to do with them. If you do not restore the land, you will have a hand in killing them."

Tecumseh paused, but kept his eyes on his adversary. Harrison could see the fire growing brighter in the great warrior's eyes. "Brother," he began again, his voice stronger and louder, "if you now offer us presents, we will not accept them, because you will later say that with them you purchased another piece of land from us! My brother and I have tried to stop the sale of land. If you will not give it up, it will produce great troubles among our peoples."

Suddenly, Tecumseh's voice rose. "The only way to stop this evil is for the red men to unite!" he declared. "We now claim a common right in the land, as it was at first and should be now. It was never divided, but belongs to all. No tribe has the right to sell, even to each other, much less to strangers."

The great voice boomed through the courtyard and echoed off the walls of the distant buildings. All sat spellbound. "Sell a country!" cried Tecumseh. "Why not sell the air, the great sea, as well as the earth? Did not the Great Spirit make them all for the use of his children?"

Tecumseh stopped. He was breathing heavily. When he continued, his voice was even and low, but everyone could hear what he said. "How can we trust the white people?" he hissed.

"When Jesus Christ came upon the earth you killed him and nailed him to the cross."

Tecumseh cleared his throat. "Everything I have said to you is the truth," he said calmly. "The Great Spirit has inspired me."

Silence lay over the crowd as Tecumseh's speech ended. Only birds chirping in the distant trees could be heard. Finally, Governor Harrison rose to give his own speech. His basic point was that the Indians could not claim to be a nation, since they were really many separate tribes. Tecumseh had no right to speak for the Miami, Sac, Fox, or dozens of other tribes. It made no sense to speak of these separate tribes working together as one nation.

Here Tecumseh interrupted the governor. "But it does make sense!" he cried. "There is a model for such a union."

Harrison frowned. "Where is the model?" he asked.

Tecumseh smiled. "Your country!" he cried. "The states have set the example of forming a union among many. Why should they oppose the Indians for following it?"

There was an embarrassed silence. Governor Harrison had no answer to this. How could he argue? The Indian chief had used the formation of the United States as a model for his Indian nation!

Instead, Harrison went on to another point. "The United States has been fair in dealing with the Indian tribes," he said. "We have negotiated legal treaties signed by chiefs."

Suddenly, Tecumseh leaped to his feet. "We will kill those chiefs!" he cried.

At this, Chief Winamac, the Potawatomi chief who had signed the treaty and who was now sitting at Harrison's side, blanched and reached for his tomahawk. Tecumseh grabbed his own tomahawk out of his belt and stood ready. Governor Harrison jumped between the two men and held them apart.

"You are both great chiefs!" he said nervously. "Tecumseh, you must realize that this chief made a fair deal with the United States. His people are happy . . ."

Tecumseh could not stand this. "Liar!" he shouted. The veins stood out in his neck. His eyes bore like daggers into Harrison. He stood massive and powerful, his arm bent to drive the tomahawk into the governor's skull.

Harrison quickly unsheathed his sword and held it to defend himself. In the ring around him, Tecumseh could hear the soldiers set their muskets. The Indians had jumped to their weapons as well.

For a moment Tecumseh and Harrison stood frozen. The formal politeness of politics had vanished and the two men stood with their true feelings shining through, feelings of hatred for a different way of life that neither could understand and that threatened them both.

Finally, Harrison breathed slowly and lowered his weapon. Tecumseh did the same. Harrison ordered his men to put away their firearms. The meeting was quietly adjourned.

The next day, Tecumseh formally apologized to Harrison for his behavior. He explained that he and his braves feared an attack. Relieved, Harrison accepted the apology and asked for another meeting. Tecumseh agreed and invited the governor to come to the Indian camp.

Harrison came that afternoon. He was still a bit suspicious as he sat on a bench. Tecumseh, however, had entirely gotten over the affair of the day before and appeared cheerful, and even playful. He promptly sat on the bench beside the governor, so close that Harrison was forced to move over. Tecumseh then gently nudged himself right up against Harrison. Again the governor had to move over. Again Tecumseh moved up against him. This time Harrison did not move but said, "Sir, you are forcing me quite off the bench!"

Tecumseh smiled playfully. "And you are doing the same to the Indians!" he said. Harrison chuckled uncertainly, then frowned.

This time the meeting was a private one. Harrison asked Tecumseh a series of direct questions. "Are you serious about your movement?" he wanted to know. He tried to explain that the United States was much stronger, that in a war the Indians would be destroyed.

In answer, Tecumseh said that he and his warriors were fully prepared to fight to the death to preserve their lands. However, he would prefer to live in peace with the Americans. He told the governor the Indians would like to join with the Americans in fighting the British in the coming war. (By now Harrison was not surprised that Tecumseh knew a war was coming.) But, Tecumseh said, if the U. S. president continued to take Indian lands, the Indians would fight with the British against the Americans.

Harrison frowned. He told Tecumseh that he would send a letter to the president explaining the Indians' position. But, he said, he was sure the president would not change his mind. The United States was committed to expansion.

"Well," Tecumseh said, "since the Great Chief is to determine the matter, I hope the Great Spirit will put sense enough into his head to make him give up this land. He is so far off that he will not be injured by this war. He may sit in his town and drink his wine, while you and I will have to fight it out."

And both men knew that this was what would happen.

The Battle of Tippecanoe

Tecumseh now felt as though there was some type of beast inside him that kept pushing him onwards. He moved with superhuman speed. He had hoped to keep his Indian alliance a secret from the Americans, but at the meeting with Harrison he had been forced to explain his position. Now that the Americans knew what he was up to, they were sure to try to prevent him from achieving the great alliance. The year 1810 was nearing its end. Tecumseh had to act quickly.

With the winds of November blowing icy gusts of air through the forests and across the fields of the north country, Tecumseh rode like a man possessed northward to Amherstburg across the Canadian border. There he held a series of talks with Matthew Elliott, a British Indian agent, to solidify the union between the English army and the Indians. Then, in a flash, he was off southward gathering support one more time.

Tecumseh wanted an Indian/British alliance

Governor Harrison, sitting in his mansion at Vincennes, was bewildered by the reports he received about Tecumseh's movements. He wrote to the War Department in Washington, D.C., about the Indian chief:

> *For four years he has been in constant motion. You see him today on the Wabash, and in a short time hear of him on the shores of Lake Erie or Michigan, or on the banks of the Mississippi. And wherever he goes he makes an impression favorable to his purpose. He is now upon the last round to put a finishing stroke to his work.*

Governor Harrison finished his letter by darkly indicating his intention to destroy the Indian alliance. "I hope, however," Harrison wrote, "before his return that that part of the work which he considered complete will be demolished, and even its foundation rooted up."

By the time Harrison wrote that letter, Tecumseh had traveled 600 miles south from Indiana and was now among the Creek and the Choctaw Indians of Mississippi, Alabama, and Georgia. He even traveled as far south as the humid lands of the Seminoles in Florida. Everywhere he went he spoke with a kind of supernatural passion, his whole body quivering with emotion as he urged—even demanded—that the Indians join his union. To each tribe he explained the coming war and the reasons why the Indians must join with the British against the Americans.

Villagers gathered and listened to this stranger from the north. He stood before them with a wild passion shining in his face. An American general who chanced to hear Tecumseh wrote, "His voice resounded over the multitude, now sinking in low and musical whispers, now rising to the highest key, hurling out his words like a succession of thunderbolts. I have heard many great orators, but I never saw one with the vocal powers of Tecumseh."

Often, though, the old chiefs just shook their heads at Tecumseh. Why should they join in the battles of the white men? Listening to such questions, Tecumseh would rise like a great thundercloud, look down into the eyes of his audience, and cry out his answer:

"Where today are the Pequot? Where are the Narragansett, the Mohican, the Pocanet, and the other powerful tribes of our people? They have vanished before the greed of the white man, as snow vanishes in the summer sun. Will we also let ourselves be destroyed? Shall we, without a struggle, give up our homes, our lands, bequeathed to us by the Great Spirit? The graves of our dead and everything that is dear and sacred to us? I know that you will say with me, Never! Never!"

And the throng would cry with him, "Never! Never!" Tecumseh won converts by the hundreds.

With the Seminoles of Florida, Tecumseh made a special arrangement. When he met with Elliott in Canada he arranged to have a ship from England, full of guns and ammunition, dock in Florida. He now explained that the Seminoles must get these arms and use them. The Indians had no calendar to help them know when the ship would arrive, so Tecumseh invented one. He did this by tying a bundle of red sticks together.

"Every morning," he told the chiefs, "you must remove one stick. When there are no sticks left, the ship will arrive." The Seminoles followed Tecumseh's orders, and when war came they were well equipped.

In Alabama, Tecumseh ran into resistance from some Creek tribesmen. They were not interested in his alliance or his war, and did not believe that they could act together with Indians as far north as Detroit. Tecumseh angrily stamped on the ground, and there was a dull thud. "Do you hear that?" he asked. "I leave here soon and will go straight to Detroit. When I arrive there, I will stamp my foot on the ground and shake down all of your houses! Then you will believe me!" The stubborn Indians scoffed and sent Tecumseh away.

A few weeks after Tecumseh left the Creeks, the villagers were astonished by a huge earthquake that shook the ground not only under their homes, but all through the south. "Tecumseh is in Detroit!" the Indians cried to one another in astonishment, believing the chief had stamped on the ground and caused the quake. It was purely a coincidence that an earthquake occurred about the time Tecumseh returned to the north, but it was good enough to convince the Creeks to join his alliance.

Tecumseh left the south feeling very good about his movement. Things were looking bright now. He had thousands of warriors committed to fighting the Americans. His great organization was in fine shape.

When he arrived at Prophet Town, however, he found a terrible tragedy awaiting him.

* * *

Governor Harrison also had been busy following the meeting at Vincennes. He knew the Indians were gaining strength with each passing day and he was determined to crush them before they got too powerful.

Harrison waited until after Tecumseh had sped south with his best warriors. Then he struck. Prophet Town was unprepared and without its great military leader. This, Harrison felt, would be the perfect time to destroy it.

On September 26, 1811, Harrison left Vincennes at the head of an army of more than 1,000 men. On foot and on horseback—loaded with supplies, arms, and stores of ammunition—the army made its way northward along the bank of the Wabash to Prophet Town.

The Prophet learned of the coming army almost as soon as it had set out. It was far too big and noisy to sneak past the Indian scouts who regularly combed the forests. But the Prophet was not a military leader. He knew the enemy was approaching, but what was he to do?

When Harrison's army had reached Burnett's Creek, just outside Prophet Town, they made camp and waited for dawn. The Prophet realized that the army was sure to attack his settlement in the morning. A party of Winnebago advised him to ride out and attack before the American army reached Prophet Town, and he finally agreed. Two hours past midnight, under cover of the forest's thick darkness, a party of Indians armed for battle set out to meet the enemy.

Harrison was fully aware that the Prophet knew of his army's presence, and he was prepared for an attack that night. He ringed his camp with sentries who sat staring into the wall of trees. The rest of his men slept with their rifles at their sides.

Just before four o'clock in the morning, a shot rang out. One of the sentries had spotted an Indian moving through the inky blackness. Instantly, the soldiers were on their feet and in position, rifles blazing. At the same moment, the forest erupted with war whoops, and the blackness was pierced with little orange sparks of the Indians' musket fire.

Now both sides had taken cover and the fighting eased into a pattern of shooting and silence. By six o'clock, the eerie light of dawn revealed that the Indians' position was hopeless. They were vastly outnumbered, and the white men were stocked with enough ammunition to continue fighting for hours. One by one the warriors faded back into the forest. Soon there was no opposition. The Americans marched triumphantly into Prophet Town.

The town was deserted. The Prophet and all his followers had fled into the forest, leaving behind all their possessions. Harrison ordered everything in sight to be burned. Watching the great Indian metropolis go up in flames, Harrison smiled grimly. The Battle of Tippecanoe, named after the nearby Tippecanoe River, was over, and he had won.

Actually, Harrison had lost more men than had the Indians. The estimates were that sixty-two Americans were killed, and about forty Indians. Although Prophet Town was destroyed, it was not a total defeat for the Indian movement since there were still tribes loyal to Tecumseh throughout the country. It was, in fact, a small battle. But Governor Harrison exaggerated his victory. He boasted to his superiors in Washington, D.C., that "the Indians have never sustained so severe a defeat since their acquaintance with the white people."

Unfortunately, Americans across the country believed Harrison. To settlers in the new lands, the Battle of Tippecanoe symbolized their dominance over the wild, bloodthirsty Indians who threatened their homes and their families. William Henry Harrison, who had done nothing more than defeat a small band of Indians and burn their town, became a national hero.

* * *

After six months in the South, Tecumseh returned to find a charred landscape. Immediately, Tecumseh sought his brother.

Furiously, he railed the Prophet for his foolish leadership. "How could you allow this?" he cried, grabbing the religious leader by the hair and shaking him while the Prophet's followers looked on in amazement. "You are no leader! You are nothing but a fool. I should kill you here and now!"

Tecumseh did not kill his brother, but he did strip him of all claims to leadership. The Prophet had disgraced his brother and the entire Indian movement with his weakness in a time of crisis. In the eyes of the Indians, he was no longer a prophet but just the brother of Tecumseh.

If Governor Harrison thought the Battle of Tippecanoe would cause Tecumseh to give up his efforts to fight the Americans, he was wrong. Fury and revenge burned in Tecumseh's heart, not despair. As he later said, remembering the day he returned to his ruined town:

> *I stood upon the ashes of my home, where my own wigwam had sent up its fires to the Great Spirit, where I summoned the spirits of the braves who had fallen in their vain attempt to protect their homes from the grasping invaders. And as I snuffed up the smell of their blood from the earth, I swore eternal hatred: the hatred of the avenger!*

16
War Is Declared

In Washington, D.C., meanwhile, a very nervous man sat in the White House. His name was James Madison. He had been Jefferson's secretary of state and had become president just as tensions between the United States and Great Britain were reaching their highest point. Madison, a cautious, wiry, thin-faced man, was about to send his young nation into its first all-out war since winning independence.

Ever since the British had admitted defeat at the hands of the colonial army in 1783, a large number of Englishmen believed that the new country would not be able to last. These men were convinced that America was too vast for a new, inexperienced government to control. In addition, the new government was far too weak. This fact the Americans themselves soon realized. In 1787 they dissolved their first form of government, a loose confederation of states that could act independently of one another, and adopted a constitution that set up a stronger national government.

Still, the British were hopeful that the United States would not last. After the American Revolution, many British troops moved north across the Canadian border. They established forts there and waited for the signal from King George to invade the new nation. There were now many conflicts in the wild western lands that had raised tensions between the United States and England. English traders from Canada continued to venture south to do business with Indians. This infuriated American officials.

But President Madison's real troubles were occurring at sea. At this time, Great Britain was at war with France. The British refused to allow the Americans to sell goods in Europe during wartime, and were capturing American ships and taking the sailors prisoner. American citizens were outraged by this piracy and demanded action.

On June 18, 1812, the United States Congress, at President Madison's request, declared war on Great Britain.

* * *

One day before the outbreak of war, Tecumseh sat across from a grizzly faced trapper who was also a British agent. Aware that war was on its way, the English were renewing their ties with Tecumseh's powerful Indian movement. The English generals in Canada felt that Tecumseh could be the key to the war in the west.

A few days later, Tecumseh sat across from another man, an American soldier with a message from Governor Harrison. The governor, too, was aware that war was coming and, following his victory at Tippecanoe, he was making a hasty peace offering to Tecumseh.

Craftily, Tecumseh told the messenger that he was eager for peace. He was tired of the fighting. The destruction of his town had taken away his taste for battle. Tecumseh also sent some of his loyal chiefs to Vincennes to convince Harrison that they had abandoned the Indian movement and were now willing to fight with the Americans.

Once again, Harrison was fooled. He wrote to his superior in Washington, D.C.: "I do believe, sir, that the Indians are sincere in their professions of peace and that we will have no further hostilities."

This gave Tecumseh the time he needed to strengthen his alliance in the crucial weeks before war broke out.

In June, as Congress was voting for war, Harrison held a great meeting of tribes in which the chiefs would pledge their loyalty to America. Tecumseh attended. An American official offered a peace pipe to the various chiefs. Tecumseh shocked the assembled chiefs—many of whom had become puppets of the American government—by taking the peace pipe and cracking it in two over his knee. Then, he rose before the assembly and spoke:

"Here is a chance for the Indians of North America to form ourselves into one great alliance and cast our lot with the British in this war!" he declared. "Should they conquer and again get mastery of all North America, our rights to at least a portion of the land of our fathers would be respected by the king. If they should not win and the whole country should pass into the hands of the Long Knives, it will not be many years before our last home and our last hunting ground will be taken from us, and the remnants of the different tribes between the Mississippi, the Lakes, and the Ohio River will all be driven toward the setting sun!"

With this speech, Tecumseh won many of the chiefs over to the British side. He then rounded up his followers and headed north to Canada. After years of planning, Tecumseh's moment of truth was at hand: The war had begun!

* * *

Seated on the grass in the Indian camp near Fort Malden, the British fort in Canada across the river from Detroit, Tecumseh listened intently while two of his warriors chattered excitedly. They had just returned from patrolling the roads south of the camp and had captured an American messenger. Eagerly, they handed over the letter the man had been carrying.

Tecumseh gave the letter to the son of the English Indian agent Matthew Elliott to translate. He then listened with mounting excitement as Elliott read the contents. A train of supply wagons was heading north to reinforce the Americans stationed in Detroit. The commander of the train, Captain Brush, was asking the American General Hull to send troops to protect the supplies, since there were only 150 soldiers guarding them.

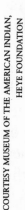

British flag given to Tecumseh in 1812

Tecumseh jumped to his feet in excitement. So far the war in the North had not gone well for the British and their Indian allies. However, all through the Ohio River Valley and deep into the South, the Indian tribes recruited by Tecumseh were fighting valiantly. They were forcing the Americans to devote their effort to fighting them rather than the British. But in Canada, neither side had proven itself superior. The Americans had sent an army of 3,000 men to invade the country, and the British and Indians could not afford to let the Americans get stronger. Tecumseh had to cut off these supplies.

The problem was that he had only twenty-four warriors. He immediately sent a messenger to Colonel Procter, the British commander, requesting troops. He couldn't wait for them to arrive, so he assembled his little band and set off for the River Raisin near Brownstown, where the supply train was to halt.

Tecumseh decided on his tactic. Since he had only a handful of men, he had to make it seem as if he had more. He therefore selected a spot along the road where the brush was thick on both sides, and he ordered his men to take positions in this dense grass. Soon they could hear the pounding of horses' hooves as the American wagons, led by 150 troops, drew near.

Tecumseh waited until the soldiers were within an arm's length. Then he shouted and his men opened fire at point blank range. The surprised soldiers turned, their horses reared, and the whole column broke in confusion. Some soldiers fired, but they didn't know where to aim. The column turned and fled down the road, leaving many of the supplies behind. Indians started to dash onto the road and give chase, but Tecumseh ordered them back. It would be foolish to let the retreating unit see that they were running from only twenty-four Indians.

When they were out of sight, Tecumseh and his men stepped onto the road. The Battle of Brownstown, as it became known, was a stunning triumph of wits over numbers. It was the first clear victory in the War of 1812 for the British army. And its hero was the Indian Tecumseh.

The Panther's Last Strike

Two men, both hardened warriors, sat together at a wooden table, their heads bent over a map.

The first was Major General Isaac Brock, a tall, broad-shouldered Englishman. He wore a red British military jacket with gold buttons and fringed epaulets. His head was balding but he remained a youthful-looking man. He was a daring and aggressive general.

The second man at the conference table was dark-skinned and had jet-black hair that flowed down over his shoulders. He wore deerskin leggings, a deerskin shirt that went to his knees, and a fringed cape over his shoulders. Attached to his belt were a silver-mounted tomahawk and a broad-bladed knife in a leather sheath. He wore a silver ring through his nose and a fluffy white ostrich feather in his hair. From his neck dangled a large, heavy medal with a picture of King George on it, a present from his English friends. His face, as he stared at the papers on the table, was creased with forty-four years of wisdom and wear. He was Tecumseh.

Brock and Tecumseh liked each other. They were both bold, confident leaders who inspired love and respect. Brock had heard many legends about Tecumseh's daring and skill as a general. Now he heard for himself the Indian chief's wisdom and intelligence.

The war had reached a crucial stage. The Americans held Fort Detroit, but they were led by General Hull. He had been a bold leader in the American Revolution but had become timid in his old age. General Brock had to decide whether to wait for reinforcements or to attack the fort now. His officers counseled him to wait. He sent them away and called Tecumseh into his quarters to ask the Indian's advice. Tecumseh uttered one sharp word: "Attack!"

Brock smiled and put his arm around Tecumseh's shoulder, leading him to the table. He, too, favored immediate action. Together, the men looked at maps of the fort and discussed how the attack should proceed. By midnight they were ready. At four o'clock in the morning, the attack on Fort Detroit began.

Tecumseh had urged an immediate attack because he knew that Hull was a weak general. He did not think the man would last long under sudden pressure. And he was proved right. No sooner did the British cannons begin blasting at the fort than a white truce flag went up. The Americans were surrendering!

Even the British and Indian warriors did not consider the taking of Fort Detroit a true battle; it was too easy. The American soldiers were furious that their weak leader had ordered them to surrender. They angrily threw their muskets on the

Tecumseh

ground and cursed Hull, while their Indian and British enemies swarmed in and took possession of the fort.

Seeing themselves suddenly the prisoners of Indians, the American soldiers turned white with fear. They had heard about the horrible tortures Indians were likely to put their prisoners through before killing them. But Tecumseh put these fears to rest. He controlled his Indians well, and none of the American prisoners of war were tortured or slaughtered. In time, the prisoners came to admire this Indian leader who lived in a room in the house of General Brock and who occasionally appeared on the streets of Detroit wearing white man's clothes. He was respectful of the captive soldiers, and when they were released, they told tales of the strange and noble Indian Tecumseh, who showed them mercy.

Now the war was going in favor of the British. Tecumseh received word of a string of small Indian victories in the south. His alliance was holding. The tribes were fighting the Americans.

General Brock, meanwhile, had assured Tecumseh that if the British won the war he would stipulate that the setting up of a permanent Indian nation west of the United States be included in the treaty. Then Tecumseh's dream would come true. There would be an Indian nation that could grow as the tribes learned to work together as one large unit. Sitting in his room in Brock's house, Tecumseh imagined the wonderful possibilities. Perhaps, he thought, their Indian nation would have a legislature to solve problems, just as the United States had a congress. Each tribe would send representatives just as the states did. For a time it looked like his dream might come true.

* * *

Soon Tecumseh rode south again to tour villages and to make sure that the Indians were indeed keeping the American soldiers busy. He was not disappointed. In the spring of 1813, he returned to Canada with new recruits. He now led an army of 3,000 Indian warriors.

When he returned to Fort Malden, Tecumseh learned to his dismay that his friend Brock had been killed in action. The new commander was Colonel Henry Procter, a stuffy man who had no love for Indians and showed it. Tecumseh and Procter did not get along.

Nevertheless, the two had to work together. Soon word came that William Henry Harrison was speeding north to

Major General Isaac Brock

attack the British at Detroit. Tecumseh convinced Procter that Harrison had to be stopped. The two leaders swept south with a force of Indian warriors and British soldiers. They surprised Harrison's forces at Fort Meigs on the banks of the Maumee River in Ohio and devastated them in a terrific battle. Nearly 500 of Harrison's soldiers were killed. Tecumseh had avenged the burning of Prophet Town.

Colonel Procter, commanding the Indians, then led the prisoners to the nearest British fort while Tecumseh remained behind. Not long after the column had set out, however, an Indian rider appeared before Tecumseh. The rider knew that the great chief insisted that prisoners be treated fairly, and he had come to report that the Indians were killing their American prisoners and Colonel Procter was doing nothing to stop it.

Tecumseh leaped onto his horse and flew northward. He charged into the unit's camp to find the Indians torturing and killing prisoners. Enraged, he rode down on two Indians who were holding a prisoner and preparing to kill him. He leaped from his horse with a terrific cry and came crashing down on the Indians. The whole camp looked up, stunned.

Then Tecumseh pulled out his tomahawk and ran around the circle of Indians and British soldiers. He dared anyone to harm another prisoner. "The next man who touches a prisoner will die!" he screamed, his face flushed with rage.

Colonel Procter came over to see what the trouble was. Spotting him, Tecumseh swore at the man and asked how he could permit such savagery.

"Sir," the colonel replied in an offhand way, "your Indians cannot be controlled."

Tecumseh nearly lifted his tomahawk and hacked the man's head off. Controlling himself, he gritted his teeth and hissed, "You are unfit to command! Are you a man? Go and put on petticoats. I conquer to save, while you conquer to murder!"

Twenty American prisoners had been killed. Tecumseh knew that word would spread of the savagery of the Indians, and this was the worst thing that could befall his movement. He hoped to build a nation that others, even the Americans, would respect. But if stories of such atrocities leaked out, the

Americans would continue to think of the Indians as little more than beasts.

Procter, meanwhile, further infuriated Tecumseh by his treatment of the Indians. At one point the army's provisions ran low and the Indians were given horsemeat to eat. Tecumseh accepted this as necessary in wartime, but when he noticed that the British soldiers were eating salted beef he flew into a rage. Seeking out Procter, he bluntly told the colonel that he would not accept such an insult. Procter wanted to ignore the problem and tried to push his way past the irate Indian.

At this, Tecumseh's wrath boiled over. He grabbed the man's collar and held him in front of him, then touched the hilt of Procter's sword and the handle of his own tomahawk. "You are Procter, I am Tecumseh," he barked. This was Tecumseh's way of saying that he was willing to fight to the death over such an insult.

Procter's face turned white. He had never understood these wild men, and had never bothered to consider that this man, this "King of the Woods" as he called him, was a military leader of great daring and skill. This challenge only strengthened his belief that the Indians were uncivilized savages. However, he backed down and ordered that the Indians be given salted beef.

Tecumseh's troubles increased during the next few weeks. Colonel Procter had witnessed the growing American military presence in the area and was slowly pulling his troops back into Canada. Tecumseh hated him even more for retreating and called the colonel "a miserable old squaw." There was little Tecumseh could do but follow the British and leave his homeland behind.

With the British in retreat, Governor Harrison led his army in pursuit. Tecumseh's anger mounted as the Indians followed the British deeper into Canada. Why did this weakling commander insist on retreating? The British had originally promised Tecumseh that they would support the Indians in their attacks on the American Northwest. But instead they were retreating. Several times Tecumseh insisted to Procter that the army turn around and fight the oncoming American forces, but each time Procter declined, saying that they were greatly outnumbered.

As his Indian army, his great alliance, moved farther from its homeland, Tecumseh found his hopes dying. The British were not fulfilling their part of the bargain. Like a fool, he had assumed that they would fight as fearlessly as his Indians. Sloshing through icy streams on his horse, marching alongside his people, Tecumseh felt his great dream of an Indian nation slipping away.

At last, when the army had reached the Thames River, Tecumseh bluntly told Procter that he and his warriors would retreat no farther. Procter called a halt and held a discussion with Tecumseh. They decided that the army would fight at this location. Tecumseh had selected this spot because it was perfect for defense. But the night before the battle, as he sat with his followers gazing into the campfire, he felt somehow cold and distant from the army. He recognized it as the feeling the Indians called "the touch of death"—the same feeling that had touched his brother Chiksika on a night before battle so long ago.

When his comrades asked what was bothering him, Tecumseh replied in an icy whisper, "Brother warriors, we are now about to enter into an engagement from which I shall never come out. My body will remain on the field of battle."

Tecumseh thought of his son, who was now a teenager living with Tecumpease. Mechanically, Tecumseh removed the battle sword he wore around his waist and handed it to one of his warriors. "When my son becomes a noted warrior and is able to wield a sword," he said, "give him this."

In the morning, Tecumseh was feeling much better. He was eager for battle. Acting without a care for what Procter would think or say, he took over command of the combined armies. Procter said nothing, but allowed Tecumseh to proceed. Quickly then, Tecumseh arrayed his men for battle. The spot was perfect for defense—a swamp was to the left of the road and the Thames River was to the right. There was no place for the oncoming army to escape.

Tecumseh positioned the British troops on the road and stretched the Indians out along the woods that bordered the swamp so that they could fire from two sides at the American lines as they approached.

Tecumseh knew that Harrison's army contained 3,000 men. The British and Indian forces, meanwhile, numbered 1,000. Nevertheless, he was in good spirits. The gloom of the night before had vanished in the expectancy of the oncoming clash. His heart was pounding with anticipation as he barked orders to the Ottawa, Wyandot, Shawnee, Kickapoo, Winnebago, Potawatomi, and Delaware Indians who had followed him devotedly and who now expected him to lead them to victory. Even though they were outnumbered, the Indians believed that they were the better fighters and therefore had the advantage. Tecumseh's eagerness infected them.

As he waited for the Americans to appear, Tecumseh went among the British lines, patting the men on the shoulder to give them encouragement, just as a British commander would have done. British soldiers who survived the battle said this gave them great comfort.

Soon the assembled troops heard a brash burst of trumpets and, looking ahead, saw the road and fields on both sides thick with charging cavalry. Harrison's mounted regiment was upon them!

The crackling of musket-fire and the boom of the one British cannon in the center of the road filled the air. Cries of pain swirled around in the wind. Tecumseh, back with the Indians, barked out the order to fire. The woods echoed with the sounds of battle.

Almost as soon as the battle had begun, however, the British troops fell back in retreat. The American cavalry came pounding after them, cutting and hacking the fleeing men. The team manning the cannon fled in terror and the Americans took possession of it. In one swift charge, Harrison had taken the British position. Seeing his men in a panic, Procter himself turned and ran.

Tecumseh's Indians, however, held their ground. They knocked the Americans back with their initial fire. Harrison ordered his cavalry off their horses and into the woods. The fighting then became more like the usual Indian warfare, with the two sides shooting at one another from behind trees.

Harrison, however, had many more men at his disposal. He kept pushing forward, forcing the Indians nearly into the swamp. The Indians kept heart though. All up and down the lines the Indians could hear Tecumseh's big voice booming commands and encouragement. One American who was in the woods firing on the Indians heard Tecumseh's voice ringing out and later described it, saying, "He yelled like a tiger."

Tecumseh was hit once, twice, but he still commanded his men. As they squatted and fired, they would see him darting among them, his deerskins dyed red with blood. The great voice kept them going.

Gradually, though, the Americans closed in. The Indians relentlessly continued firing. Suddenly, they realized that the voice was no longer barking orders. There were only cries of agony and the crack of muskets. Finally, faced with surrender or escape, the braves slipped away one by one through the forest.

As the daylight ended on October 5, 1813, the Americans found that they had won a complete victory, and, in the process, they had killed Tecumseh. The Battle of the Thames was finished, and so was the dream of an Indian nation.

* * *

Tecumseh's body was never found. At least, it was never found by American or British forces. Tecumseh's closest companions said that they had taken his body into the forest and buried it. But some people were not completely convinced. From time to time, someone would claim to have seen the great chief alive. But this was impossible, for if he had lived, he would have continued to work toward an Indian nation.

Without Tecumseh, the tribes had no strong force to keep them together. They returned to their old ways, and over the next several decades their remaining lands were steadily taken from them.

As for Colonel Procter, he was later brought before a military court and charged with cowardice in battle. Fourteen of the men under his command testified that in his retreat into Canada and in the Battle of the Thames he did not act in the best interests of his men and of Great Britain. One of the charges was that in the battle "his attempts to rally the men and support the Indians were insufficient, and that he prematurely quit the field." Procter was court-martialed. He died eight years later, in disgrace.

William Henry Harrison, the victor in the Battle of the Thames, went on to run for president of the United States. His running mate was John Tyler, and they campaigned with the slogan "Tippecanoe and Tyler Too." The image of the Battle of Tippecanoe as a great victory of "civilization" over the Indians stayed in the minds of Americans. People considered Harrison a hero. In 1841 he was elected the ninth president of the United States. Harrison died during his first year in office.

Americans of the nineteenth century revered the men who defeated Indians and made the land safe for settlement. Among people of that time, the dreams and deeds of the Indian chief Tecumseh were largely forgotten. But, strangely enough, Harrison himself recognized Tecumseh's greatness and wrote of him: "If it were not for the vicinity of the United States, he would perhaps be the founder of an empire that would rival in glory Mexico or Peru."

In 1816, three years after Tecumseh's death, the Indiana Territory became a state. Although its citizens continued to fear Indians, they could not deny the greatness of the Shawnee chief who had once caused them such fear. A few years after the Battle of the Thames, a newspaper in Vincennes summed up the truth about Tecumseh:

> *He was truly great—and his greatness was his own, unassisted by science or the aids of education. As a statesman, a warrior, and a patriot, take him all in all, we shall not look upon his like again.*

Suggested Reading

Cooke, David C. *Tecumseh: Destiny's Warrior*. New York: Julian Messner, Inc., 1959.

Edmunds, R. David. *Tecumseh, and the Quest for Indian Leadership*. Boston: Little Brown & Co., 1984.

Johnston, Johanna. *The Indians and the Strangers*. New York: Dodd, Mead & Co., 1972.

Josephy, Alvin M., Jr. *The Patriot Chiefs*. New York: Viking Press, 1961.

The Council on Interracial Books for Children. *Chronicle of American Indian Protest*. Greenwich, CT: Fawcett, 1971.

Tucker, Glenn. *Tecumseh: Vision of Glory*. New York: Russell & Russell, 1973.

ADVANCED READING:

Icenhower, Joseph B. *Tecumseh and the Indian Confederation 1811–1813: The Indian Nations East of the Mississippi Are Defeated*. New York: Franklin Watts, Inc. 1975.

Thom, James Alexander. *Panther in the Sky*. New York: Ballantine, 1989.